PHOTOGRAPHS
OF THE
UNKNOWN

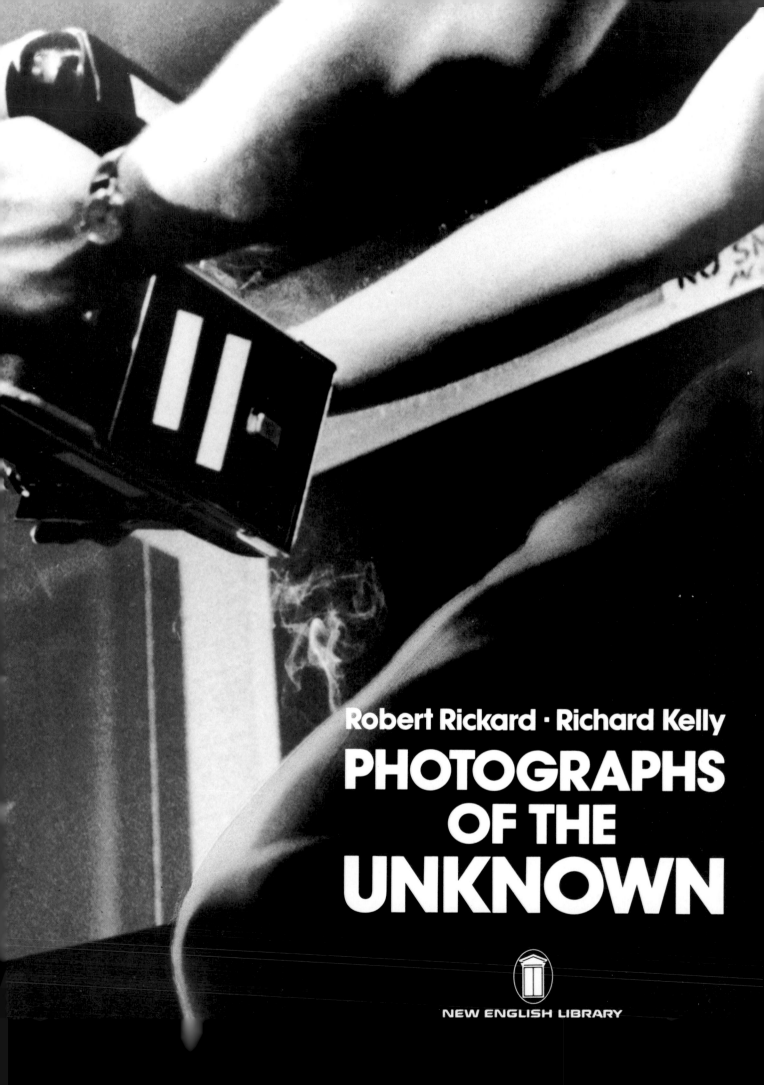

Robert Rickard · Richard Kelly

PHOTOGRAPHS OF THE UNKNOWN

NEW ENGLISH LIBRARY

Half-title In 1936, a professional photographer, Mr Indre Shira, was commissioned by Lady Townshend to take a series of pictures of Raynham Hall, Norfolk. As Shira and his assistant set up their equipment, a "vapoury form" came down the stairs in front of them. Shira had the presence of mind to release the camera shutter before fleeing.

Title spread Ted Serios, of Chicago, Illinois, produced hundreds of pictures by projecting his concentration onto photographic film (see pp.80-81).

ACKNOWLEDGEMENTS

Every effort has been made to trace and credit the copyright owners of all photographs appearing in this book. In cases where this has not been possible, copyright owners should contact Granta Editions Ltd for inclusion in subsequent editions.

The authors would like to express their sincere and grateful thanks to the people and organizations who made this book possible.

To the following for their advice and readiness to help locate photographs: James Bolen, editor of *New Realities;* Charles Bowen, editor of *Flying Saucer Review;* Gordon Creighton; Hilary Evans of MEPL; Patrick Ferryn, editor of *Kadath;* Joseph H. Golden; Gerard Lebat, editor of *Les Extraterrestres;* Geoffrey Lake for translating material; Cyril Permutt; Pam Riva of *Psychic News;* Clair Schwarz of *National Enquirer;* José Melendez of Agencia EFE; Alexander Low; Mr Kato; and Souvenir Press for their permission to use Guy Playfair's material.

To the following for lending us material from their own collections, and for going out of their way to provide prints at short notice: David Barritt; Janet and Colin Bord of FPL; Raymond Lamont-Brown; Romano Cagnoni; Peter Costello; George & Nancy Clamp; John Cutten; Douglas Dickins; Alaister B. Frazer; Fritz Goro; Robert J. Greenler; Chester H. Heath; Benson Herbert of the Paraphysical Laboratory, Downton, Wilts; Frank Lane; Stella Lansing; Jim Lorenzen of APRO; B.T. Matthais; Roger Mitchell; Steve Moore; Graham Morris for his unique coverage of the Enfield poltergeist; Dr Thelma Moss; the National Meteorological Library at Bracknell, Berks; S.C. Neame; Rev. Julian North; Our Lady of Roses, Mary Help of Mothers Shrine, Bayside, New York; Harry Oldfield; Ann & Bury Peerless; Guy Lyon Playfair; Mrs D. Puri for the amazing Sai Baba photos; Antonio Ribera; Eileen Roberts; Robert P. Sharp; Harry Oldfield; Brian Snellgrove; William Spaulding of GSW; Richard Veilleux; Major Colman VonKeviczky of ICUFON; Jeff Watson; Gerry Bennett; Dr B. Heuvelmans; and Judith Luckwell.

We are also deeply indebted to the following for their enthusiastic and generous co-operation which made the book a pleasure to work on: Michel Bougard, who sent over 300 UFO photos from the files of the Belgian group SOBEPS; Dr Jule Eisenbud; Gladys Hayter for her readiness to share her discoveries; August C. Roberts who pulled off a miracle getting material to us from his unique UFO collection; Dr Berthold E. Schwarz whose enthusiasm in providing photos and contacts forms one of the pillars of this book; and Jun-Ichi Takanashi whose selfless and prompt response brought forth some of the many gems in this book.

Finally, we are deeply grateful to Sam and Pat for their encouragement, patience and help during the various stages of this book and dedicate it to them.

First published in Great Britain in 1980 by New English Library Ltd.

Produced by Granta Editions Ltd in association with
Book Production Consultants, 7 Brooklands Avenue, Cambridge.

First NEL Paperback Edition 1981

NEL Books are published by
New English Library Ltd.,
Barnard's Inn, Holborn,
London EC1N 2JR.

ISBN: 0-450-04991-4

Designed by Richard Kelly

Printed and bound in Spain.

CONTENTS

INTRODUCTION

In this wonderfully varied existence of ours there are many things which continue to defy disbelief. Fortunately many of us harbour a secret suspicion that unidentified creatures still roam forests and sport in lakes and seas; that UFOs and phantoms are not the products of swamp-gas, the bottle or mental illness; and that strange forces are working beyond the cocksure ken of dogmatic scientists. These sympathies are very real and vitalize a realm of high drama and archetypal themes: it is a war zone in which human aspirations and dreams are pitted against objectively real necessities all along the shifting frontier between the known and the Unknown. We hope this book borrows some of the spirit of modern photo-journalism in presenting the camera as a witness to some of these skirmishes.

It is not easy to take photographs of things which are not supposed to exist, or which are dismissed as figments of over-excited imaginations. You don't just go out and photograph the 'impossible'. Nevertheless such photos continually arise: products of the chance meeting between the photographer and something out of the ordinary.

The early life of such evidence of unusual or paranormal phenomena is perilous, because it has to survive a number of formidable and unexpected obstacles. The very subject matter of the photo is often under vigorous dispute and the photographer faces the possibility of ridicule as a crank or dismissal as a lunatic. We can consider, then, only the material offered for public scrutiny by brave individuals. We hope that this book will encourage many others to come forward, especially since the general attitude to photographic evidence of the paranormal is turning to one of eager investigation.

Paranormal Photographs – Who Cares?

Since 1882 the prestigious Society for Psychical Research (SPR) has investigated the claims of spiritualism and allied phenomena, in which time it has remained very cautious about spirit photography – understandably, since many of its leading members have been branded as gullible when a medium they have endorsed was exposed as a trickster. The great folklorist, Andrew Lang, who became president of the SPR in 1911, refused to even consider such photographs although he studied all other aspects of the paranormal.

Nevertheless there has been a strong current of serious interest. In 1918 Lang's contemporary, Sir Arthur Conan Doyle and a group of professional photographers, some of them unconvinced about spirit photos, set up the Society for the Study of Supernatural Pictures (SSSP). In its short life it obviously satisfied a public need and was sent a great many interesting photos, the whereabouts of which we were unable to discover. Two of these are still popular

1 The main workshop of Harry Price's National Laboratory of Psychical Research, founded in 1925, as a base for his well-publicised ghost hunts.

2,3 On 23 April 1960, veteran Nessie hunter Tim Dinsdale filmed a mysterious wake moving in the distance on Loch Ness. This enlargement [left] was compared with the wake of a motorboat filmed at the same distance from Dinsdale's boat [right]. Both sequences were examined by a military reconnaissance unit in 1966 and again in 1980, and pronounced to be very strong evidence for the existence of a large unidentified creature, of which only a protruding hump could be seen.

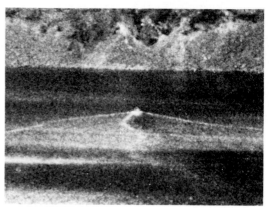

today: the famous fairy photos taken by two young girls, Elsie Wright and Frances Griffiths, of Cottingley, Yorkshire; and the much travelled alleged portrait of Christ (p.94:2). In 1920 the SSSP announced its successful experimentation with psychic photography, but regretably did not elaborate further.

Today, psychic research has been heavily institutionalized and is regarded as thesis material at, mainly American, universities able to support dedicated teams with sophisticated equipment, laboratory space and computers. Harry Price, perhaps the most famous ghost hunter of the first half of our century, founded his own National Laboratory of Psychical Research in London in 1925 [1], setting the pattern for numerous individuals and energetic groups. Despite their limited facilities they still produce research to match that of the universities; but they really come into their own in on-the-spot case investigations.

The position is much the same in the field of UFO investigations. There have been several university-based study programmes, but these have been accused of severe bias because they were motivated by military and political funds. Again the mantle of research has fallen upon the shoulders of individuals and small groups like Dr Allen Hynek's Centre for UFO Studies, in Evanston, Illinois, and numerous national and local UFO groups in nearly every country of the world.

Virtually every aspect of the unusual and paranormal has its dedicated following of serious open-minded investigators – like monster hunter Tim Dinsdale [2,3] and many others who painstakingly gather what information they can (see pp. 14-25). There is another group who call themselves Forteans – after Charles Fort (1874-1932), an American writer, philosopher and iconoclast, and pioneer of the collection and study of accounts of all the phenomena included in this book – whose view is that every event or phenomenon interrelates with others, and that we need to develop more inclusive ways of looking at and interrogating the Universe before we can start to make sense of its answers. There are a number of Fortean organizations, and independent magazines like *Fortean Times,* which exist to promote research into all the

above topics and to disseminate the results.

All of these various parties have looked into alleged photographs of the phenomena that interests them. There is a commendable spirit of mutual co-operation between them – eg. Ground Saucer Watch, a civilian group which specializes in computer analysis of UFO photos (pp.60-61), has also looked at the Cottingley photos and some of the Loch Ness Monster – but no attempt at the co-ordination or integration needed before orthodox science will accept these efforts with the seriousness they deserve.

The Perils of Paranormal Photographs
But before we have any photographs at all of paranormal phenomena, the person with the camera has to be in the right place at the right time – a rare event in itself when we are dealing with erratic, anomalous, short-lived and unexpected events. Next, our lucky – or some would say, unlucky – photographer has to have his wits about him. A cull of the literature would reveal many hundreds of cases in which witnesses were too startled or paralysed to reach for their cameras – or were so absorbed in watching that they didn't remember the camera until too late. And, of course, during the excitement the operation of a camera, especially a sophisticated one, can be bungled – the main reason for the badly framed, out of focus and under or over exposed views of UFOs, sea-serpents and ghosts familiar to us all.

A further stage in the hapless life of photographic evidence is the high incidence of camera malfunction at the critical moment – a detail confirmed by many a witness or investigator of UFO, mystery creature or psychic phenomena – and other calamities.

According to Guy Playfair's account of the Enfield poltergeist (see pp.140-143), in *This House is Haunted* (1980), he and fellow investigator, Maurice Grosse, were literally bedevilled by their tape-recorders which jammed, stopped recording, and once became stuffed with unwound tape. The photographer on the case, Graham Morris, who made an unparalleled pictorial record of the poltergeist at work and its effect on the family [4,5], also had to contend with inexplicable jinxes on the automatic cameras left at the house. Similar interferences and interruptions occurred to many of the cameras which took the photos in this book.

But worse can happen as our valuable evidence is further depleted by unfortunate losses. In 1874, Sir William Crookes, the physicist, took a series of 44 pictures of the full-body materialization of a spirit entity called Katie King (see pp.108-109). Most of them were destroyed, and sadly only a few tatty examples remain of one of the most remarkable records in the history of spirit photography.

A more detailed case in point is the evidence for the Loch Ness Monster, which has been the object of consistent photographic attention since the first photo of Nessie in 1933, by Hugh Gray (p.15:5), which was the only one of a whole roll to turn out well. The disaster list includes: Malcolm Irvine's ciné film, of December 1933, lost, as was a second film, taken in September 1936, of which only a few stills remain; only two of the four shots taken by Kenneth Wilson came out (p.14:1,2), and the original of one of these was lost, leaving only a poor print; a ciné film taken by a Dr Macrae in the early 1930s has been mislaid; and a film taken by C.E. Taylor in 1938 has never been allowed a public showing by its trustee. More recently Doc Shiels' portraits of Nessie (p.14:3,4) suffered the same fate as those of Wilson — the original colour slide of the second shot vanished *en route* to America.

So the casualty list grows of valuable photographic evidence damaged beyond salvation, destroyed in accidents, and simply mislaid through neglect or the passage of time. But for any one of the foregoing factors, we should have had indisputable proof of the baffling phenomena which taunt us to solve their riddles. It makes us very grateful for the survival of the evidence we were able to locate, and for our opportunity to present the photos to you with as much clarity and colour as possible.

The Background – Photography and Spiritualism

There is no specific moment in history we can pinpoint and say: "The story of strange photography starts here." Throughout history paranormal phenomena have been incorporated into works of art in every medium, from the illustrations of fantasy, mythology and religion, to the representations of actual events. From the moment of its discovery — Nicephore Niepce's first true photographs were taken in 1822 — photography was used to record every facet of human experience.

It would be difficult to find a comparable and completely new technology that was adopted so rapidly at every level and profession in society. Its special magic became a familiar tool for scientists, explorers, journalists, and even artists and

4 In a remarkable series of photos, Graham Morris documented the poltergeist that disrupted the life of the Harper family, of Enfield, London. Shortly after the disturbance began in August 1977, Morris, taking this photo was nearly hit by a flying brick, which Mrs Harper [left] is dodging.

5 As objects were flying around the front room, three of the Harper children (left to right: Pete, Janet and Rose) became steadily more alarmed. (See also pp.140-143).

ordinary folk, capturing for posterity anything odd that crossed their paths. Reflecting this widespread interest, magazines and newspapers became photograph-hungry, and some initiated special features as a showcase for the oddities sent in by readers. For example the 1894 volume of the *Strand* magazine reflects a typical diversity of techniques: a photo through a beetle's eye, a decapitated mule still standing, a 'ghost', an aerial photo, photos of stars through telescopes, a bullet frozen in flight, and a close-up of a fly's tongue. Regular favourites of *Strand* readers were vegetables shaped like animals or humans, the bizarre tricks of lightning, things found inside eggs, vegetables or trees, and bibles or cigarette-tins etc. which had saved their owners by stopping a bullet.

The history of photography itself only takes off in the last half of the nineteenth century; a time of ferment and consolidation accompanying the expansion of science and Empire. This dynamic period from the publication of Darwin's *Origin of Species* in 1859 to Freud's equally consequential first work on psycho-analysis in 1895, saw wave after wave of innovation affect every member of society: votes for women, and education as a child's right; developments in railways, industry, astronomy, chemical and electromagnetic physics, medicine and surgery; Bell's telephone, Marconi's telegraph and Rontgen's x-rays. But most importantly for us, this celebration of materialism stimulated a predictable reaction — the rise of spiritualism which soon developed its own applications of photography. After all, what better way to show the existence of spirits than to make them visible in a photograph?

Spiritualism, in itself, was nothing new – similar practices and phenomena are recorded in the shamanistic traditions of all peoples, and seem to be an instinctive expression of psychic forces in the basic nature of man. Archaic societies integrated this instinct into their social structure – but modern man has divorced this side of his nature, repressing it in favour of 'scientific' materialism, an imbalance that affects us all individually. Modern spiritualism, surely an unconsciously collective movement towards balance, is reckoned to have begun with a poltergeist haunting of a house in Hydesville, New York, when the Fox family moved in, in December 1847. The house had a reputation for disturbances, and the family had a history of somnambulism. Soon family life was severely disrupted by knockings and movements of furniture, among other forms of mediumistic phenomena, which centred on the two young daughters, who developed a technique of question-and-answer with what they were fully convinced was a discarnate entity. From this beginning grew the nuclear ritual of medium and séance, and the belief that the spirits of the dead could communicate with the living in numerous ways: by speaking through the entranced medium, by a disembodied 'direct' voice, or by materializing in an ectoplasmic body.

A Brief History of Psychic Photographs

Photographing ghosts was not an obvious idea. It began with an accident and only seriously came to worldwide attention when the first professional spirit photographer, William H. Mumler, was prosecuted in New York City for fraud. Mumler, of Boston, Massachusetts, told the court that in 1861 he had borrowed a friend's equipment to take a self-portrait, focusing it upon a chair, uncapping the lens and then rushing over to pose in the chair for the prescribed exposure time. On development of the glass negative plate he was amazed to find a female form superimposed [6]. As news spread, Mumler gave up his old occupation as an engraver to take portraits full time, offering the bonus attendance of the sitter's deceased friends and relatives. He fled to New York in 1867 after a scandal in which some of his alleged phantoms were recognized as living Bostonians. Soon after taking up his new occupation in New York, the luckless Mumler was arrested after complaints were made to the Mayor. Although he was acquitted after dozens of satisfied customers testified on his behalf, he was effectively ruined and died in poverty in 1884.

Once publicized, the idea of spirit photography became obvious and eager experimenters extended the range of subject matter to other invisible notions of the day, like ectoplasm (pp.74-75), the human aura (p.75:2) and even attempted to capture images of thought. Within several years of Mumler's trial the

pioneers, Edouard Buguet in Paris and Frederick A. Hudson in London, were well established.

Buguet's photographs are regarded as masterpieces of contemporary photography, even without the 'extras', as the phantoms became known, and visually superior in every way to Mumler's crude efforts. Unfortunately Buguet made a sudden public confession in 1875, that he had tricked everyone with double-exposure. Like Mumler he had many supporters – many of them men of high esteem who could not be called gullible – who protested that Buguet had satisfied the conditions of many a strict test, producing recognizable images of the departed. There is strong evidence that Buguet was the victim of a conspiracy to discredit spiritualism in its most vulnerable form. Certainly spirit photography never recovered any credibility after this double scandal.

But however easy it is to dismiss the work of such men and their successors, a careful examination of the records of their trials, denunciations or alleged exposures tends to show the case against them was far from proved, and usually motivated by an unsavoury prejudice, character assassination, and arguments based upon false logic. A close study of the subject reveals that the issue is a good deal more complicated than the simple question of whether the medium cheated or not. There were many mediums of genuine abilities – like Eusapia Palladino (p.126:2) – who resorted to tricks as their talents waned. Others had abilities which were unreliable from the start, and used small deceits to bolster their own confidence as much as their audience's, until the authentic power took over. There are those whose psychology makes them unwitting accomplices to unconscious fraud, like children in a genuine poltergeist case pathetically trying to remain the centre of attention as the disturbances become less frequent. And still others find themselves deserted by their powers in the presence of hostile or sceptical investigators, which naturally confirms the latter's suspicions. It is a state of affairs an investigator into any aspect of the paranormal has to learn to cope with.

A further complication is the extraordinary degree to which our subjects suffer from coincidences. The sceptic will dismiss a meaningful coincidence as mere chance, without being able to say what chance is. As Charles Fort once observed, there never was an explanation that didn't need to be explained itself. Coincidences enrage the rationalists yet relate very much to the individual who experiences them, very like a poltergeist. One example occurred in 1908, when F.C. Barnes came from Australia to London to visit the spirit photographer Richard Boursnell, and was told of the presence of a beautiful spirit lady. The ageing Boursnell was reluctantly persuaded to

6 The first recorded spirit photograph, taken by William Mumler, of Boston, in 1861. He wrote: "This photograph was taken by myself, on a Sunday, when there was not a living soul in the room beside me, so to speak . . . The form on my right I recognize as my cousin who passed away about 12 years since."

7,8 We have identified hoaxes where known, but investigators have to be eternally vigilant. This impressive photo of a UFO emerging from the volcanic crater of Mount Aso, in Kyushu, Japan [left], was discovered, by the Modern Spaceflight Association, a leading Japanese UFO investigation group, to be a double-exposure using a local brand of fluorescent light fitting [above].

indulge in his former pursuit and took a photograph of Barnes. The Australian, expecting to see the form of his dead wife, found to his dismay that he did not recognize the figure at all. Much later, Barnes discovered that the image was a replica of a portrait in the frontispiece of a book he had seen sometime before, which had much impressed him.

It is easy to criticize the facility most of us have for seeing patterns, figures and faces in the most unlikely places. Yet, as John Michell proved in *Simulacra* (1979), such phenomena are distinctly 'synchronistic' – to borrow the psychologist Carl Jung's term for meaningful coincidences – involving the simultaneous participation of the human imagination and the forces of the physical world. Indeed this is the same prescription as 'psychokinesis' the name given by psychic researchers to the hypothetical mind-over-matter force which manifests spontaneously as poltergeist phenomena (pp.136-143), or under the control of conscious or unconscious mediums, appearing in a range of phenomena from levitation to apports and metal-bending (pp.124-135).

Yet another mystery is encapsulated in the problem of spirit photos – are they true photographic images? In 1892 J. Traill Taylor, a distinguished member of the Photographic Society of Great Britain, and then editor of the *British Journal of Photography*, embarked on a series of strictly controlled experiments with Scottish medium David Duguid, whose reputation was untarnished by the usual suspicions. Taylor, while not outraged by the question of paranormal phenomena, wanted to resolve matters one way or the other, if only for the sake of his profession and personal interest. Among many cross-checks and controls, Taylor installed more than one camera in the séance room – a technique later used to good effect in the 1920s by Dr T. Glen Hamilton to record the full range of mediumistic phenomena (p.106:7,8). Much to his consternation, Taylor reported to the Society, 'abnormal appearances' were found on many of his plates in spite of his precautions. After examining the discrepancies with his equipment, including a stereoscopic camera, Taylor deduced that the images were not formed through the lens, suggesting that they might be 'crystallizations of thought'.

Taylor's conclusion, that 'the psychic image might be produced without a camera', had been demonstrated for a fact by mediums up to the present day. William Hope, championed by Conan Doyle throughout the 1920s, many times demonstrated an ability to perform 'psychic writing' on any designated plate in an unopened pack brought by investigators. Stanislawa Tomczyk (pp.128-129) could put 'psychic lights' on sealed plates some distance from her hands. Olga Worrall, one of America's most respected mediums today, affected a fresh piece of film by holding it (p.74:5). It was developed immediately and said to show an image of ectoplasm, the substance exuded from mediums from which psychic structures and materialized spirits are constructed.

This demonstrable link between mind and matter supports the theory of poltergeists proposed by Dr Nandor Fodor in the 1930s, that they seem to be associated with certain mental states of the focus or victim of the activity, and that

9 In 1972, Uri Geller was on his way from London to Munich for another demonstration of his psychokinetic ability to bend metal. He claims that his camera repeatedly levitated off his lap, pointing out of the plane window. Taking the hint, but seeing nothing outside the window he shot a few frames, which later showed these UFO-like shapes. The merging of several different kinds of phenomena in a single event is typical of many paranormal happenings.

unconscious forces in the mind can sometimes find expression by influencing, psychokinetically, physical events. A spontaneous example of this occurred when Mrs Ardis Schwarz was most worried about her father (p.139:4).

Interestingly, the above incident happened during the visit to the Schwarz household of Stella Lansing, a Massachusetts housewife who found strange images on her ciné films (pp.182-83) following a close encounter with a UFO. And soon after his study of Stella's phenomena, Dr Berthold Schwarz found images developing on his own films (p.92:5). Very often the presence of someone who is himself a conscious or unconscious medium, is enough to trigger the talents of another latent medium. Buguet needed a mesmerist's passes for his photos – and Frederick Hudson's spirit photography began in March 1872, when the well-known physical medium, Mrs Agnes Guppy, paid a visit to his studio. Similarly immunity to pain and heat sometimes seems dependent on the shamanic figure who presides over some forms of firewalk (p.120:1).

We are presented then with several alternatives for the mechanism of psychic photography. The primary one – that the camera, plate and lens somehow made invisible things visible – was discredited but recently reprieved through the use of special films. Gladys Hayter, a contemporary medium training for 'direct voice', produced phenomena on an orthochromatic infra-red film (p.79:5,6) – while another example (p.103:4) used a special full colour infra-red film on which the colour red indicates a heat source, green indicates radioactivity, and blue electromagnetic radiation. Secondly, there is the suggestion that mediums can and do produce ectoplasm, which under certain circumstances can be objectively photographed (pp.74-77 and 106-110).

Thirdly, we have Taylor's question, as posed by Charles Fort in 1931 "whether the human imagination can affect a photographic plate?" The evidence today rests mainly on studies and experiments in 'thoughtography', which we illustrate with selections from the results of Ted Serios, Stella Lansing, the Veilleux brothers and the work of Professor Tomokichi Fukurai (pp.80-85), and the more spontaneous effects from a variety of people and conditions (pp.92-95). Support for the idea of 'thoughtography' comes from the real ability of some people to move or levitate objects without touching them (pp.124-125 and 128-129], a psychokinetic power which might extend to influencing the molecules of the film emulsion. And if this is true, even the preposterous Cottingley fairies might be rehabilitated as the 'thoughtograph' of the young girls' conception of fairies.

The reader can make his own choice, but it would not be prudent to rule out situations in which different combinations of these or other forces may be acting. Besides entertaining you, we hope this book will stimulate some of you to experiment, or at least keep your eyes open and camera ready. If you get results, let us know.

Towards a second volume
In researching this book we looked through most of the historical and contemporary archives available to us which might have contained material of interest. Despite the rarity of the material more accumulated than we could practically include. We had to make some hard choices in our selection from the dozens of subjects and hundreds of photos. We concentrated on strong visual themes, but in order to do full justice to our selection we regrettably had to leave out many deserving subjects and fascinating photos. Other splendid material arrived too late for inclusion. We consoled ourselves with the promise that if the response to this book was favourable, and we had the opportunity, we would certainly have enough material for a good second volume to complement this one.

For that reason, and partly because of our own continuing interest in the subject of paranormal photos, we would be interested to learn of new material. Numberless photographs of strange phenomena must be languishing forgotten in drawers or old albums, probably because their owners feared disbelief or ridicule. To these people we offer a fair hearing, a sincere interest, and a chance to show the pictures to the world – anonymously if they wish. We hope this book will encourage them to come forward with their photos. Such visual evidence is urgently needed if our understanding of the neglected mysteries around us is to make any real progress.

Accordingly, we would like to extend an invitation to any reader or his friends who know of, or possess puzzling photos which would not be out of place in a book like this one. If you are willing to submit your photograph for examination and consideration, for a possible second volume of PHOTOGRAPHS OF THE UNKNOWN, the authors would be grateful if you would contact them via the address given on page 144.

Bob Rickard – Richard Kelly

STRANGE
LIFE

In 1912, an aviator, stranded on the Indonesian island of Komodo, discovered a hitherto unknown species of giant lizard. These Komodo 'dragons' are aggressive, carnivorous and can grow up to 10ft (3m) long.

Loch Ness. The first ever clear photo of Nessie's head was taken in April 1934 by a London doctor, R. Kenneth Wilson [1]. Wilson took another three shots of which only one survived, showing the creature diving [2]. On the morning of 21 May 1977, Anthony 'Doc' Shiels snapped her twice from the grounds of Urquhart Castle [3,4]. Unfortunately, like Wilson's evidence, all that remains of one of the photos is a poor copy print [4] taken from the colour slide before it was lost in the post. Doc said: "The part of the neck showing above the waterline must have been around four or five feet . . . I could see no eyes . . . the light patch above the 'mouth' is a reflection off a kind of ridge."

Nessie was photographed for the first time in November 1933, by Hugh Gray, a local man who had seen Nessie before. Only one of his shots survived the jinx [5].

In December 1975, Dr Robert Rines unveiled the first underwater photo of Nessie [6]. The neck is estimated to be 10ft (3m) long and a bulky body extends back into the murky peat-laden water. Sir Peter Scott publicly named the creature *Nessiteras rhombopteryx,* or 'the Ness monster with a diamond-shaped fin'.

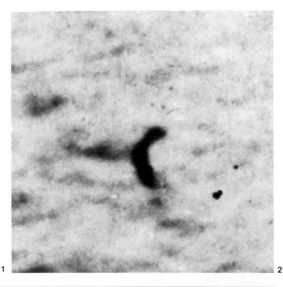

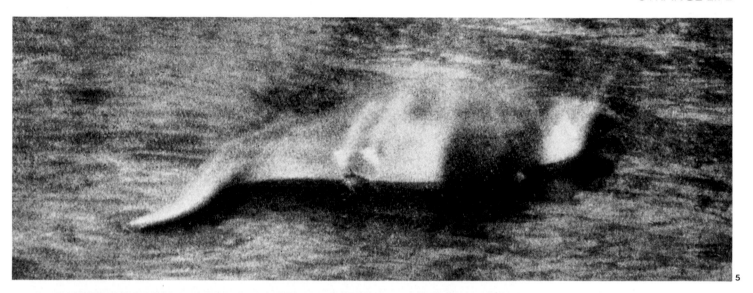

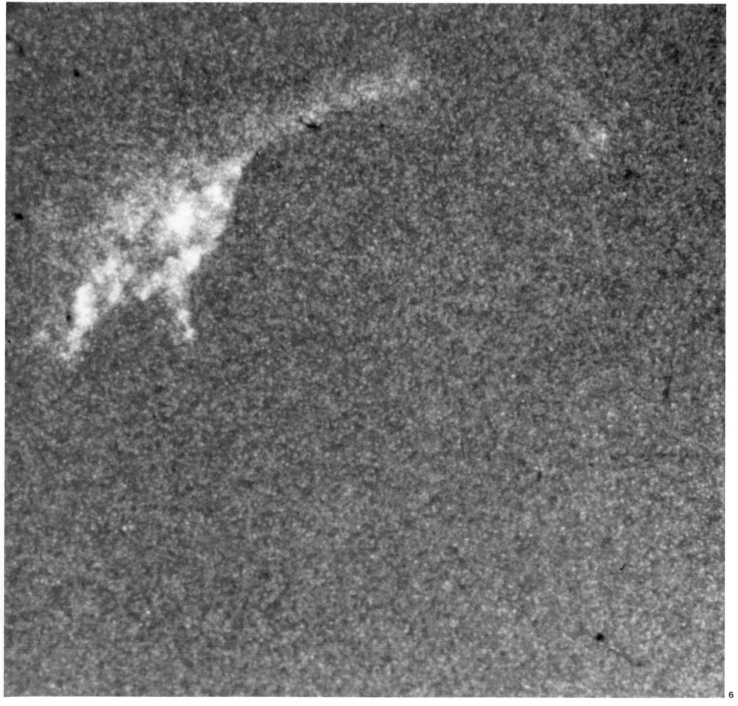

STRANGE LIFE

Loch Ness. In the early morning of 15 June 1951, Lachlan Stuart, a woodsman living on the southwest bank, his wife and another witness saw a creature in the Loch with a sheep-like head on a long dipping neck, but recent analysis of Stuart's photo [1], suggests three creatures moving in formation.

Another photo, usually said to show two creatures, is more likely to be of a double-humped monster moving at 9-12 mph towards Urquhart Castle [2]. It was taken by P. A. MacNab, on 29 July 1955.

A more puzzling picture was taken by Mrs Jesse Tait and friends, of Inverness, on 16 August 1969. She saw something moving and snapped it [3]. Some experts have suggested the disturbance was created by one or more boat wakes, but the friends are certain they saw six humps.

Enlargements of a sequence taken by a dedicated monster hunter, Jeffrey Watson, on 3 September 1978 show an underwater object moving at 10mph [4-6]. Jeff was observing, just north of Foyers, when the wake moved diagonally across the Loch towards Inverfarigaig.

4▲   5▼

6▼

Water Monsters. On 28 February 1934 this bizarre carcase [1] 20ft (6m) long, was found on the beach at Querqueville, Normandy. Press and experts speculated that the creature might have been a whale, a seal or a sea-cow, or an unidentified monster. Dr Georges Petit, of the Paris Museum, conducted a post-mortem and fairly quickly and certainly identified the carcase as that of a basking shark. He pointed out that the gill slits of this particular shark extend almost right around the neck, and on decomposition the lower jaw drops away along with most of the neck flesh, fins and abdominal organs. The result is a very plesiosaur-like carcase. This is one of the possible identities of the New Zealand carcase (see p.20).

The lakes of Canada and the USA teem with monsters. This animal [2] snapped by two fishermen on Lake Manitoba, Canada, on 12 August 1962, was described as like "a large black eel . . . swimming with a ripple action . . .".

Japan has its own Nessie — in this case Isshiee who lives in Lake Ikeda on Kyushu island. This portrait of her [3] was taken on 16 December 1978 by Toshiabi Matsubara, at about 1pm.

Since 1976 at least, there have been numerous sightings of a creature, or creatures, in the area of Falmouth Bay, Cornwall — called Morgawr, Cornish for 'sea giant'. These two photographs [4, 5] appear to show a large double-humped shape that is heading up the Helford River and then back out to sea again. They were taken early in the morning of 31 January 1977, by a local man, Gerry Bennett, who was convinced it was not a rock or something moving with the tide. The first photographs of Morgawr were taken by 'Mary F.' from Rosemullion Head, early in February 1976 [6, 7]. She was shocked by the incident, wishing to remain anonymous, but estimated the creature's length at 15ft (5m).

4

5

6

7

Sea Monster. On the morning of 25 April 1977, a Japanese fishing vessel, the *Zuiyo-maru* owned by Taiyo Fisheries, found a strange carcase in its nets as it trawled in waters about 30 miles east of Christchurch, New Zealand.

Forensic opinion was that the animal had been dead about a month. The carcase was about 33ft (10m) long; the skin had been washed off as it putrified, and parts had dropped away. Fatty tissue had decomposed into solid but friable white adipocere, torn in places to reveal red muscle tissue. It smelt so bad the crew had to throw it back – but not before acting section chief Michihiko Yano had taken these four photographs [1-4] and annotated his sketch with measurements [5].

News of this amazing discovery was not given to the media until 20 July, and immediately speculation was rife on the creature's identity. Guesses ranged from a basking shark (see p.19), and a giant sea-lion to a giant shell-less turtle. The hot favourite, of course, was some kind of marine plesiosaur – a conjectured relative of Nessie – which somehow still survived in unknown areas of the vast ocean.

In September 1977, a symposium on the problems of identifying the creature was held in Tokyo and attended by specialists in comparative anatomy, immunology, mammology, oceanography and marine paleontology – but the learned gentlemen admitted they were unable to slot the animal into its proper place in the scheme of things. The only physical evidence of the creature was some fibres taken from its fins, but they were quite ambiguous. Ironically, the creature had some affinities with all the animals suggested but if it was a shark, or turtle, or plesiosaur, it was not one known to present-day scientists.

STRANGE LIFE

The Yeti. Throughout the mountainous regions of Central Asia there is a firm and ancient belief in a giant hairy man-ape. The natives of Tibet, Nepal and northern India will re-affirm their beliefs to any traveller, and alleged relics of the creature are valued by priests – like this Yeti 'scalp' held by the head Lama of Kumjung monastery, Tibet [1].

Apart from eye-witness accounts there is very little reliable evidence of the Yeti. As in the case of Bigfoot (see pp.24-25) most of the photographic evidence is of footprints which, also like its American cousin, vary considerably in size and shape. At least two species of Yeti have been suggested, inhabiting different terrain at middle and high altitudes.

These large bi-lobed prints, found in the Menlung glacier by the 1951 British Mount Everest expedition, show a characteristic bipedal gait [2], belying the suggestion they were goat tracks enlarged by melting snow. On the same expedition, Eric Shipton photographed a much more convincing print [3, inset top], which baffles zoologists still.

On the Soviet side of the Himalayas the Yeti is taken seriously. Russian Yeti hunter, Igor Burtsev, compares his foot with the plaster-cast of a print he found recently in the Pamir mountains [4, inset bottom], where the creature is called an 'Alma'.

Bigfoot. Sightings — which number in thousands and date beyond the days of the settlers to the traditions of the early American Indians — describe a giant man-like creature covered in hair, living in the wild mountain forests of North America. Whole families of these *sasquatch,* or Bigfoot, have been reported, though usually only a lone forager is seen. Conclusive evidence is scarce because the terrain is difficult and remote and the creature is a swift and expert woodsman who steers clear of human habitations.

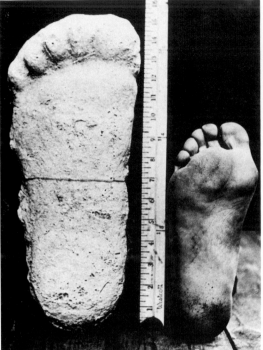

Other evidence consists of hairs, remains of meals, droppings, tape-recorded calls and footprints. This cast of a footprint [1] was found at Bluff Creek, northern California, shortly after Roger Patterson shot a unique ciné film [2] of a creature he surprised in the same area on 20 October 1967. The concensus of opinion after much analysis is that the film is genuine.

Thousands of casts of footprints have been gathered over the last century and show a bewildering variety of sizes and toe configurations. This curious print [3] — 16½in (420mm) long and believed to be deformed — was found at Bossburg, Washington, in 1969. A bizarre 3-toed print was found by UFO investigator Stan Gordon [4] at the scene of a UFO-type close encounter at a farm at Greensburg, Pennsylvania, in October 1973, involving Bigfoot-like creatures.

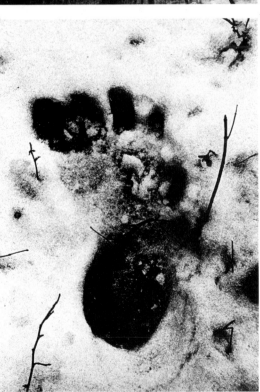

In this photo [5, inset] Bigfoot hunter Rene Dahinden stands beside an accurate sculpture — by fellow hunter Jim McClarin — of one creature 8ft (2.5m) tall.

2, 5

UNUSUAL NATURAL PHENOMENA

A classic 'UFO' photo – the impressive object is in fact a luminous lenticular cloud, photographed near Holloman Air Force Base, New Mexico, in October 1957.

Living Rocks. According to the folklore of most lands, rocks are not inert lumps of chemicals but living beings capable of feeling, movement and growth. These beliefs are very much alive today – for example, we are asked to believe that these two stones began life the same size [1].

In the north-western corner of California's Death Valley National Park, is a mystery that has puzzled geologists and sight-seers. The moving rocks of Race-track Playa criss-cross the narrow 3 mile (4.8km) long, normally dry, lake bed with their tracks.

Robert P. Sharp, of California Institute of Technology, began his observations in 1969, when he realized this well-known phenomenon had never been systematically studied. He staked the positions of 25 rocks, ranging from mere pebbles to boulders [2], and returns regularly to measure their progress. One rock travelled 212ft (64m) in several slides; others moved shorter distances, and still others converged [3] or changed direction [4]. Earthquakes, geo-magnetic disturbances, the H-bomb, and even inscrutable tricks by UFO pilots have been blamed. Sharp himself favours a combination of wind and ice – if the conditions are right a thin layer of water freezes on the flat playa overnight, then hurricane-force winds channelled through Death Valley, push the rocks on the slick surface. But no one has actually seen the rocks move and Sharp admits that all the theories to date are little more than speculation.

4▶

Falls. The annals of meteorology are full of accounts of strange falls. Most European countries have been favoured by red or orange rains. One fell on London on 1 June 1968, leaving residues of fine powder which, experts said, was Sahara sand [1], carried in the atmosphere by powerful winds.

Occasionally one hears of hail storms of extraordinary severity – like this destruction of Omaha, Nebraska, on 18 May 1936 [2] – or sufficient to bruise humans caught unawares, as in this incident in Calcutta [3]. Hail the size of eggs – these fell in 1929 [4] – can tear the wings off light planes and kill livestock. Some of the largest true hailstones have weighed well over three pounds.

More mysterious, and dangerous, are the falls of large sheets and chunks of ice. On 25 March 1974, Mrs Nonin Wildsmith was cleaning her car outside her home at Pinner, London, when an ice-bomb smashed into it [5]. Estimates from the fragments [6] indicate a diameter of about 18in (46cm), perhaps larger, since other pieces hit nearby roofs. It is usual to blame ice falling from airplane wings or toilet discharges, but this is rarely proved because of today's sophisticated de-icing equipment and the regulations regarding discharges over cities. Besides, there are many authenticated falls of ice from before the first airplanes.

6

Falls. There are many accounts of artifacts and enigmatic objects falling from clear skies. One of the strangest occurred at Rockhill, Missouri, on 14 May 1959, when a red-hot chain fell onto a bulldozer, startling its driver [1].

Joseph Barbieri points to a billboard, in New Haven, Connecticut, through which he saw a fiery object crash, in 1953 [2]. Barbieri says he watched in astonishment as the object rose again into the sky and was lost to view – which seems to rule out 'meteorite' as an explanation. Analysis of fragments, believed to be from the object, showed they were almost pure copper!

Some of these mysterious falls have been linked to UFOs. This nickel tube [3] was found at the site, in Madrid, Spain, where the 'Ummo' UFO was said to have briefly touched down in 1967 (see p.56).

In a number of cases witnesses have seen material falling, or ejected, from UFOs. Fibrous shreds, dubbed 'Angel Hair', which quickly dissolved on falling to earth, were observed at Ichinoseki, Japan, in October 1957 [4]. This substance [5] is all that remained of 'silver foam' which an old lady saw spill out of three UFOs over Campinas, Brazil, in December 1954. The foam was found to be largely composed of tin. Masses of soft metal foil [6] – looking like radar-jamming aluminium chaff – was found several days running at a New Jersey UFO sighting location.

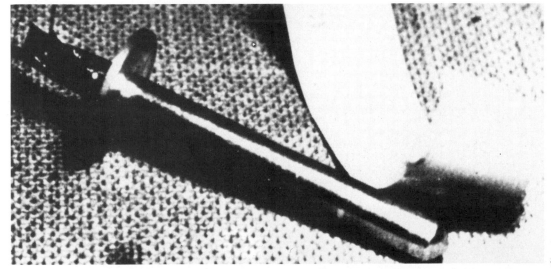

4

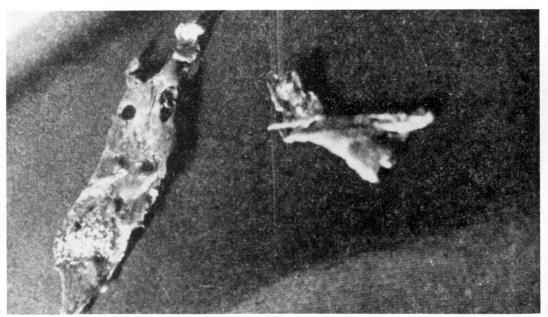

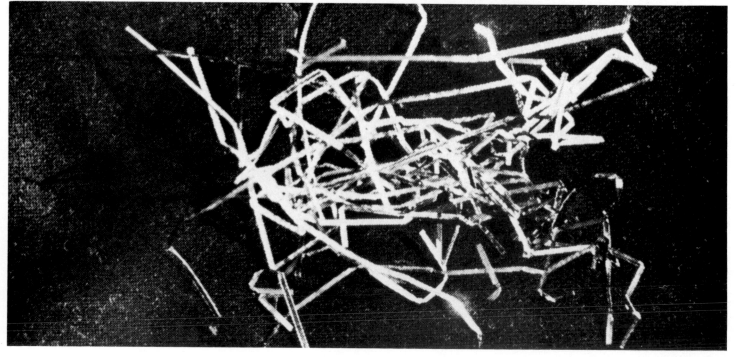

Atmospheric Magic. The optical tricks of our atmosphere still fill observers with superstitious awe or appreciative wonder, even though the physics of the event has long been understood.

Mirages can float cities into the sky and allow men to walk upon water. The men in this mirage at Puget Sound [1], in fact, stand on a bank beyond the yacht, their legs elongated and feet below the horizon, distorted through differently heated layers of air.

A 'glory' forms when the observer's shadow is reflected from banks of uniform water droplets; it is a cousin to the rainbow, and often called a fogbow. A glory is only visible from the observer's vantage, as in this beautiful example in the mists of Mount Emei, in China [2]. One variant of the glory is the 'Brocken Spectre', a greatly magnified shadow accompanying the glory, and named after the German mountain where it became infamous as a portent of doom for mountaineers. Equally famous in its own right is the form of 'Brocken Spectre' seen in Sri Lanka, the breathtaking spectacle of the huge shadow cast by Adam's Peak at sunrise [3], often with its own glory. But the most perfect glory is reserved for aerial travellers lucky enough to catch the shadow of their plane upon suitable clouds [4].

The UFO-like arcs and mock-suns of the parhelia are also universally regarded as portents. They form around the sun – seen here from the South Pole [5] – when the light is refracted through air laden with hexagonal ice crystals.

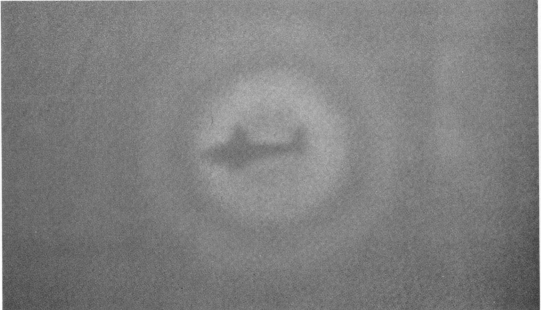

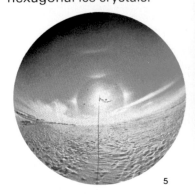

5

Natural 'UFOs'. There are many sources of light in the sky which can be mis-interpreted as UFOs — though not all UFO sightings are explicable in these terms, as we shall see in the next chapter. About 90% of all sightings have natural explanations, and a major proportion of these in turn have their origins in misidentified natural phenomena.

Meteors glow brightly on entering the earth's atmosphere, heating up as they streak across the sky before burning up and falling to earth. This meteor, photographed blazing across southern USA on 24 March 1933 [1], was 25 miles (40km) high and had a head 6 miles (9km) across.

Satellites are another source of UFO sightings. In this photo, August C. Roberts had managed to capture himself and the passage of the communications satellite Echo 1 over New Jersey [2], with a time-exposure. Similarly, clouds of barium gas, released by rockets for studies of the upper atmosphere, often lead to wide-spread UFO reports. This barium cloud [3] was seen over New Jersey in May 1967, and this [4] over Wallops Island, Virginia.

Observers have also been startled by strange luminous cigar-like clouds (see pp.26-27). This lenticular lee wave cloud was photographed in north Wales, in August 1960[5].

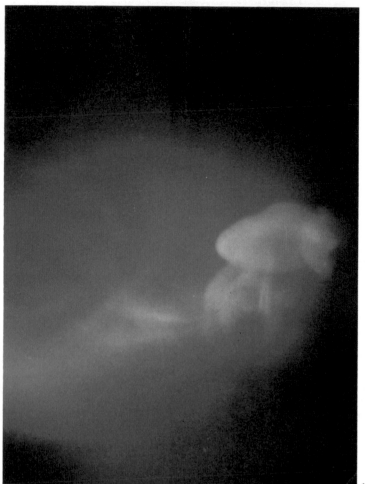

Natural 'UFOs'. The aurora borealis, or Northern Lights [1], are created when charged particles from our sun come into contact with earth's magnetic field. These impressive displays can be brief and violent, and breathtakingly beautiful, sometimes taking on strange shapes and forms which can mislead even the seasoned observer.

Far less common are the peculiar forms of lightning which both appear and behave like certain kinds of UFO sightings and photographs. In August 1961, two scientists at Los Alamos, New Mexico, recorded this strange 'pinched' or beaded lightning [2] – the first time they had seen anything like it in years of lightning photography.

Perhaps the major candidate for the title of 'natural UFO' is the phenomenon of ball lightning, whose existence is not fully accepted by some scientists, even today, because of the great rarity of objective evidence. Nevertheless, we have many records of authentic sightings by responsible witnesses and accounts of the peculiar poltergeist-like behaviour of these 'balls of fire'. Scientifically studied and accepted photographs of ball lightning are rarer than the phenomenon itself. This example was taken by Prof. J.C. Jensen, in 1933 [3]; and a more recent photograph [4] was taken by Dr D.R. Tomkins of Wyoming University in 1965. Compare these with alleged photos of ball lightning on pp.40-41.

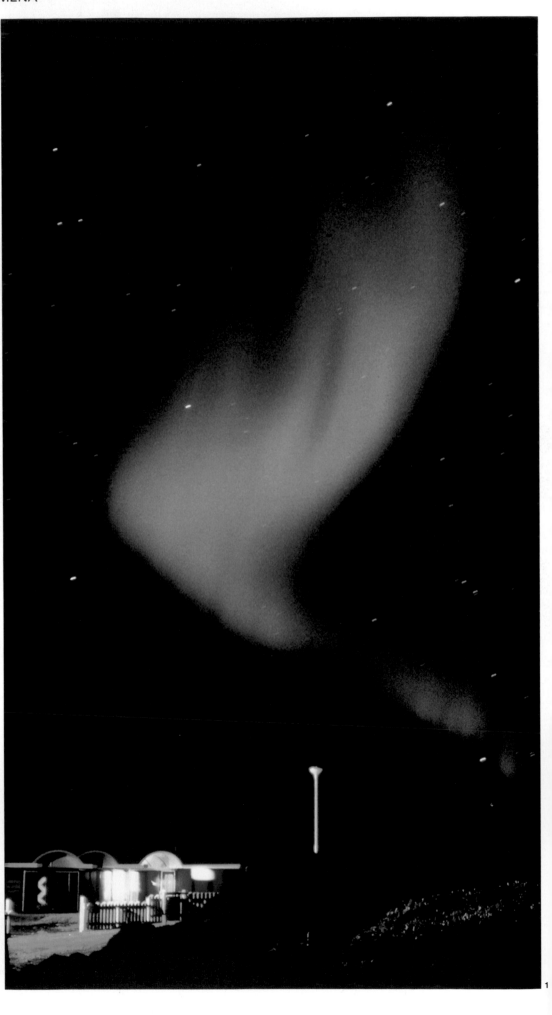

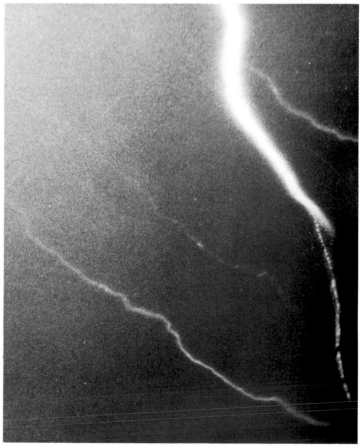

4

Ghost Lights. This strange ball of light [1] has baffled investigators of since it was taken in the zoological gardens of Basle, Switzerland, in 1907.

In June 1977, Mr S.C. Neame, of Essex, felt oddly cold as he took this picture of his wife in their living room, using a flash, and later discovered a misty ball on the colour slide [2]. The next two photos come from Chester H. Heath, of Georgia, who photographed Indian signs on trees and rocks with a Polaroid camera, only to find them obscured [3, 4]. A medium told him they were 'spirit lights' and indicated nearby treasure.

This photo was taken inside a small chapel in Kerizinen, Brittany, France, on the site of a series of BVM apparitions (see p.92) to a peasant woman, which began in 1938, with a vision of a ball of fire [5].

Seemingly inexplicable streaks of light, appearing spontaneously in photos, have been blamed on UFO's or spirits. Similarly the effects in this photo [6], taken during one of the vigils at Bayside, New York, at which Veronica Leuken has visions of Christ and the BVM, is said to be of divine origin.

A photo, taken during a storm at Castleford, in Yorkshire [7], is said to show the track of a ball lightning; but it does not compare well with known photos of ball lightning (see p.39).

However, it seems more likely that these light streaks are the result of movement of the camera or light source during exposure.

1

5

3

4

7

On the night of 8 August 1978, Pieter Roos, a worker on a communications tower in Johannesburg, South Africa, set up his camera high on the tower for a time exposure of the city, and discovered he had caught a UFO.

UFOs

Flying Cigars. In January 1964 a tight security blanket fell on a region near the town of Mendoza in western Argentina. According to rumours a widely witnessed UFO had lost speed and crashed in the Andean foothills with its crew of tiny men in luminous uniforms. Somehow, a correspondent to the respected UFO journal *FSR* obtained a copy of one of the photos [1], showing the crashed object, measuring 13 ft (4 m) in length. This mystery has not been resolved.

Belief in UFOs as physical craft from other worlds in space flourished in the 1950s, and led to numerous claims of meetings with space-people. The most famous of these 'contactees' was George Adamski who successfully photographed numerous UFOs in close-up – including this 'mother-ship releasing scout-craft', in March 1951 [2-4]. Later, in 1952, Adamski said he met their occupants in the California desert.

In July 1967 there were many reports of ''a great shining silver bar'' which hovered for three days in the sky over Cumberland, Rhode Island. The sightings attracted Joseph L. Ferriere [5], editor of the now defunct UFO journal *Probe.* Ferriere went hunting for possible ground traces on 3 July and suddenly saw the object himself, estimating its length at 200 ft (60 m). As he took a sequence of photos [6-8] he noticed a curious in-out pulsation of one end of the object (left in photos).

44

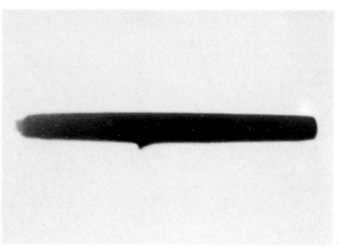

6

7

8

UFOs and Planes. UFOs have had a strong affinity for planes, being photographed near them, seen chasing planes and even allegedly causing a few aerial disasters. This photograph of a UFO over the Japanese air base at Hya Kuri, was taken on 10 October 1975 by Osamu Tsugaane [1]. During World War II, there were reports of balls of light pestering fighter pilots – these were photographed over Germany in 1943 [2], and resemble 'ball lightnings' (see pp.38-41).

In September 1957, the Martin Aircraft Company, of America, photographed a test flight of its new B-57 bomber near Edwards Air Force Base, for a publicity brochure – but to their dismay found themselves in the middle of a controversy over the true identity of what appears to be a UFO in the top right corner [3, 4].

While on holiday with his family at the Argentinian resort of Las Grutas, on the Rio Negro River, 'Franciso X' heard a peculiar humming, early in the morning. From their hotel window the family saw and snapped this UFO [5, 6]. It was about 980ft (300m), away and about 13-16ft (4-5m) in diameter.

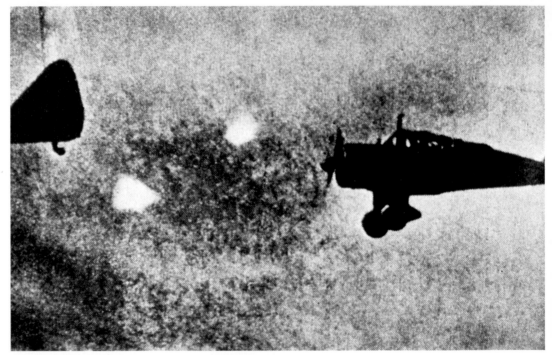

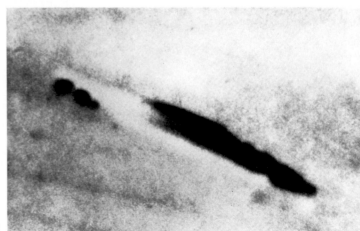

5▲   6▼

UFOs

UFOs Over Water. During January 1958, the *Almirante Saldanha,* a Brazilian naval training ship, undertook a research trip for the International Geophysical Year. On 16 January, while off the Brazilian coastal island of Trinidad, one of the crew, Almiro Barauna, took a series of photos of a 'Saturn' shaped UFO, which cruised over the headland and accelerated out to sea [1-3].

Also in Brazil, these UFOs were photographed in mid-April 1970, at Crique D'Urca, near Rio de Janeiro, by Eduardo Stokert. Note the reflections in the water which have moved in relation to the city lights [4, 5].

This lyrical photo of a UFO over a suburb of Bangkok, Thailand, was taken by Japanese tourist Akiteru Takao, 24, on a cruise up the Mae Nam River, on 7 March 1973 [6].

James Pfeiffer, an American businessman was in a small riverside restaurant north of the town of Ipamari, Brazil, on 8 May 1966, when he saw this object hovering above the trees on the opposite bank and had time to take a photo before it sped off [7].

6▲

7▼

UFO Shapes. UFOs form a cavalcade of fascinating shapes – no two appear exactly the same.

Japanese schoolboy Hitoshi Tanaka took this photo on 3 April 1974, at Kanmon Bridge, Shimonoseki [1]; and in 1951, youths point to three classic discs in the sky over Patterson, New Jersey [2].

Very little is known about this triangular UFO, seen over Madrid, Spain, 5 September 1968 [3], compared to a fairly detailed account given by witness Mike Lindstrom and his wife about the UFO they photographed while holidaying in Hawaii [4]. They snapped it from their hotel-room window, on the east side of Kauai island, on 2 January 1975. It seemed to be a bright sphere with a square platform around its middle, and made no sound.

This mechanical-looking UFO was photographed at Yorba Linda, California, on 24 January 1967, by 'Tom X' [5]. A vaporous ring was left behind by a hat-shaped UFO seen at Santa Ana, also in California, on 3 August 1965 by Rex Heflin [6].

Agusto Arranda wanted to take scenic shots high in the Ancash mountains near Yungay, Peru, on a trip in March 1967. When the prints returned from developing in Lima, Arranda showed little concern over the mysterious objects he had snapped. The UFO research organization, APRO, investigated, and endorsed their authenticity [7].

On 3 November 1973, the 'Jimenez' family, out driving near Cocoyoc, Mexico, saw this strange shape [8]. It landed not far away on the leg-like protrusions, but the family became frightened and drove off without taking any more photos.

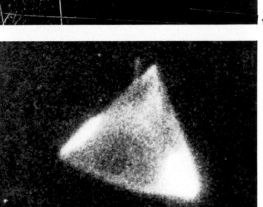

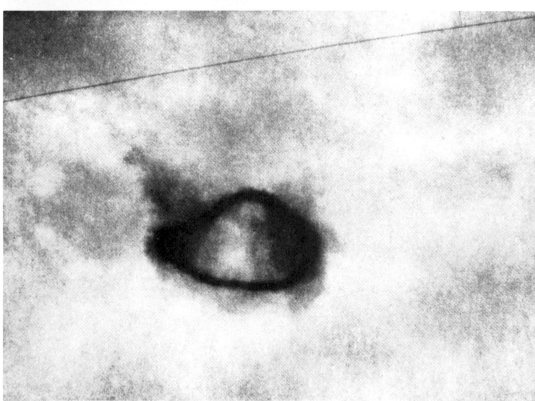

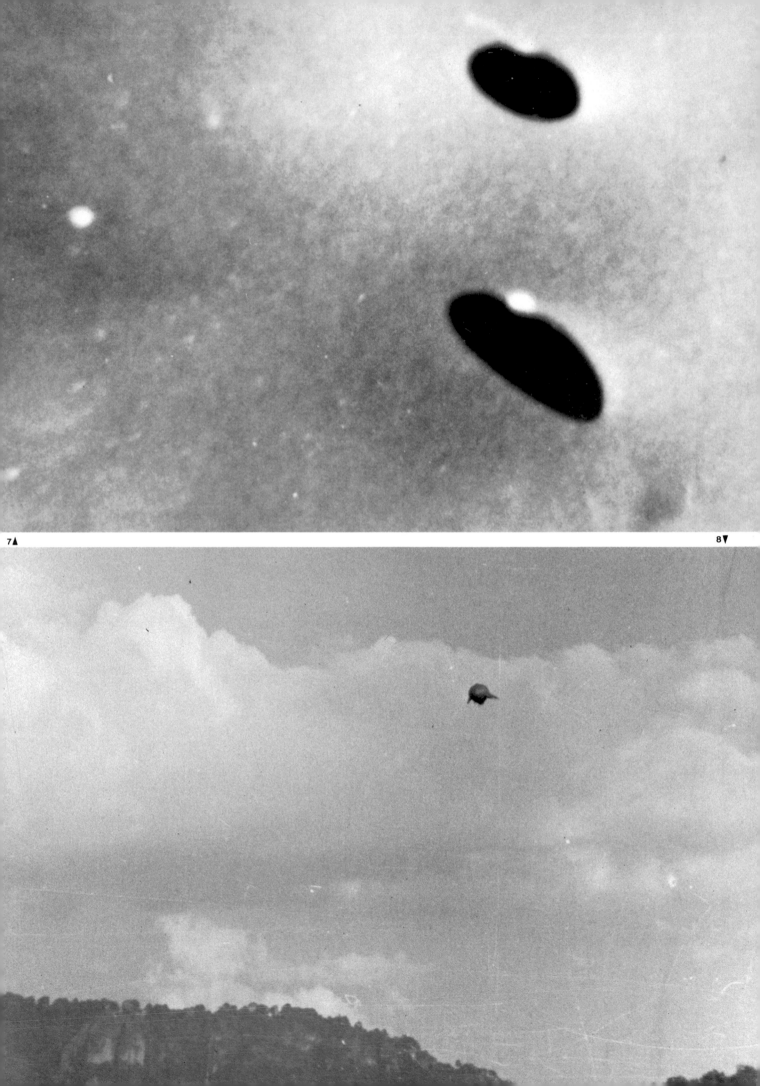

UFOs Above Us. On 23 May 1971, Rudi Nagora and his wife, of Munich, were driving among the mountains at St Lorenzen, Austria, when they noticed an object in the clouds. Rudi took a series of 12 photos – of which we show two [1, 2] – which were studied and pronounced genuine by the German UFO research group DUIST. The couple watched the UFO for a few minutes, then it suddenly vanished.

While flying at 4,000ft (1220m) over Fujisawa City, Japan, Shinichi Takeda had a clear view of this object for about two minutes [3]. After he had taken his photograph the glowing silver shape turned and sped out of sight.

Not much is known about this, one of the clearest photos of a UFO we have seen, and printed here for the first time anywhere [4]. It was sent to UFO investigator August C. Roberts by the man who took it, Jim Bjornstad, a church minister in Wayne, New Jersey, and was taken around 1970.

This unusual and battered image is said to be a photograph of a very bright UFO in the night sky of Pennsylvania, taken in 1960 [5]. The UFO was shooting down powerful beams of light into a lake or reservoir.

5

UFOs in Motion. On the night of 30 August 1951, the sky over Lubbock, Texas, was brightened by a fly-past of luminous balls, which were also tracked on radar. One of these formations was caught by Carl Hart [1].

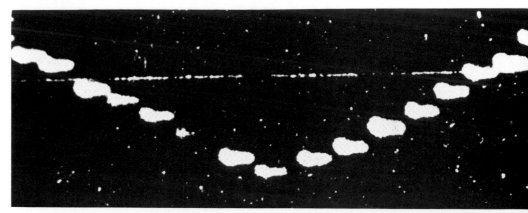

Lars Thorn stopped his motorbike when he saw something moving to and fro in the sky near Lake Vattern, Sweden, on 6 May 1971 [2]. He managed to take two photos of the domed, multicoloured object. The dark area on the right is the wall of a bomb shelter in the foreground.

A farmer at Puerto Maldonado, Peru, photographed this enigmatic UFO travelling low, in July 1952 [3].

On the last leg of a flight from Spain, over the jungles of Venezuela, an Avena Airlines pilot, approaching Maiqueta airport, snapped this disc speeding along below his plane, in 1963 [4]. He refused to divulge any more details because of ridicule from his colleagues.

Engineer Paul Paulin took a time exposure of the Paris skyline on the night of 29 December 1953, and later discovered the UFO [5].

Police sergeant Yoshiyuki Matsuda investigated a traffic accident on the outskirts of Nagai City, Japan, on the night of 9 July 1973. As part of his duties he took photographs of the scene, and at least one of these photographs recorded the appearance of a glowing object moving in the sky [6]. There were no streetlamps to cause reflections and some of the crowd appear to be looking up at the UFO.

3

5▲

6▼

UFO Beings Among Us? A complicated case occurred in Spain, when, on 1 June 1967, a curiously marked yellow UFO performed an aerial ballet over the San José de Valderas suburb of Madrid, before briefly landing in nearby Santa Monica in full view of a café full of people. Many people in the fields at San José saw the object and some photographed it [1-4]. But stranger still, was the fact that many of the people at the café were members of a space-flight discussion group who had received an announcement of the date and place of the landing several days before, and had gathered in expectation.

Antonio Ribera and his colleagues, Spain's leading UFO investigators, discovered that the mysterious communications came from a group who called themselves 'Ummo', who had been sending documents through the post and making long late-night phone calls to a number of people in Spain. These untraceable communications described the Ummo planet, in orbit around a star, 'Iumma', which they identify as Wolf 424 on our star maps. Others outlined in elaborate scientific detail the complexities of Ummo science. But all the documents were authenticated by an odd seal – a thumbprint [5] bearing a symbol similar to the marked UFO. The Ummo people said they had lived on earth since landing in France in 1950 – an event which seems to check out – and were only interested in helping mankind to maturity. Fantastic truth or elaborate hoax – no one has yet solved the enigma of Ummo.

It is believed that many experiences of contact with UFO beings go unreported for fear of ridicule. Few would endure the scorn faced, for example, by Joe Simonton, a chicken farmer of Eagle River, Wisconsin, who claimed he was given several 'pancakes' by the occupants of a UFO that landed in his backyard in April 1961 [6].

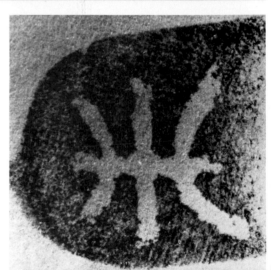

UFOs

Optical UFOs. Coastguard Shell Alpert did not intend a hoax. On 16 July 1952 he looked out of a window at the USCG station at Salem, Massachusetts, and saw these UFOs [1]. Being a photographer he snapped them, but later analysis showed that he had been fooled by a reflection of ceiling lights on the window.

The most common of the honest errors in UFO photos is an effect called a 'lens flare', caused by reflections within the lens tube – like this suggestion of a UFO created by flaring from the sun [2]. Lens flares appear only on development of the film; and the flare image is usually linked to its source diagonally through the centre of the film image area – a clue which can be obscured if the photograph is cropped.

This formation of UFOs, buzzing the Capitol, in Washington DC [3], is said to have been taken on the night of 19 July 1952 and supported by dozens of eye-witnesses and radar sightings, was in fact taken in 1965. Analysis by dedicated investigator Major Colman Von Keviczky proved these UFOs were inverted images of the balcony lamps [4].

During a skywatch on 28 July 1952, in New York, August C. Roberts took this photo [5] which critics have dismissed as a classic lens flare. But the solution is not that simple – three people saw an orange UFO which may be hidden by the photo's central glare.

3▲   4▼

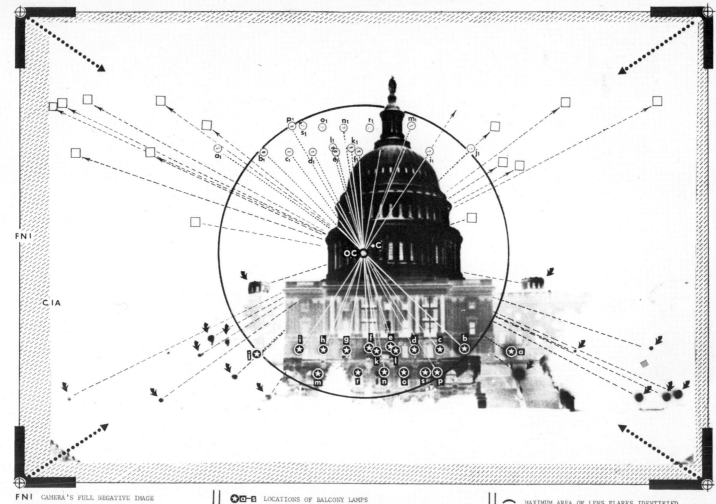

Computer Analysis.

According to his testimony to the US Air Force commission on UFOs at Colorado University – the 'Condon Committee' – farmer Paul Trent [1], of McMinnville, Oregon, was called into his backyard by his wife and together they watched an object in the sky. Trent fetched his camera and took two photos, which the Condon committee agreed were 'consistent' with the sighting report.

Ground Saucer Watch, of Phoenix, Arizona, undertook a computer analysis. One of Trent's photos [2] was divided into tiny columns – 512 horizontally and 480 vertically – making 245,760 'picture cells'. The grey value of each cell, or dot, was measured on a scale of 255 divisions between black and white by a scanning TV camera, and the data fed to a computer.

The value of each cell was then manipulated by the computer – filtered out at a selected density [3], and the contrast increased to clarify the original image [4]. Similarly, the computer compares the values of adjacent cells and enhances or suppresses moderate tonal changes, resulting in an emphasis of any edges in the picture [5] – a method that provides visual confirmation of shape, density and reflectivity, and usually shows up the wires or strings of hoaxes. The computer can also colour areas of the image sharing a similar set of values [6, 7], thereby emphasizing contours of particular interest.

Ground Saucer Watch concluded that the photo genuinely portrayed a large UFO, about 65-98ft (20-30m) in diameter, some distance away in the sky.

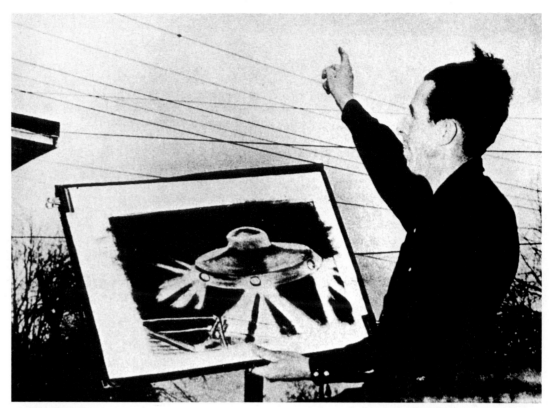

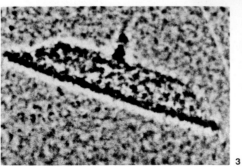

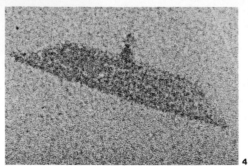

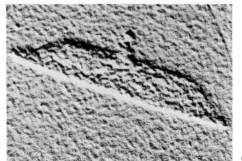

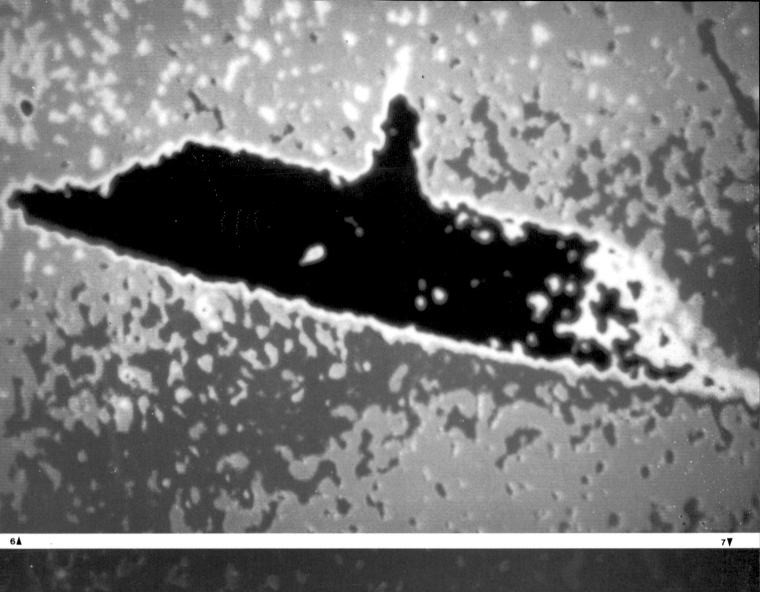

6▲

7▼

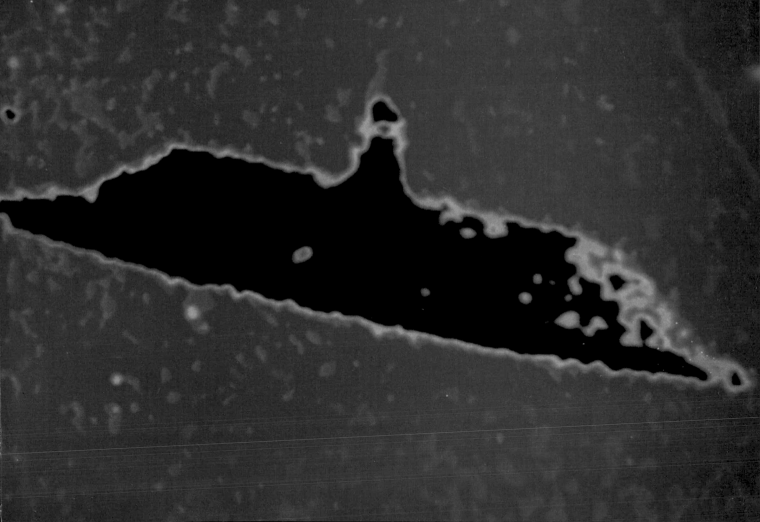

UFOs From the Sea. The Canary Islands have been the scene of many dramatic, well-witnessed UFO events in recent years, and the Spanish government has formed an encouraging relationship with serious UFO investigators.

In researching for this book we were excited to learn of a recent case which had been independently photographed by at least three people. The incident occurred on the evening of 5 March 1979, and our sequence of photos was taken by Antonio Gonzales Llopis, 26, who had been photographing views of the island of Gran Canaria. At 6.45pm Llopis noticed a peculiar effect in the sky, looking like a swirl of light [1]. Suddenly, a huge dark object surged from beneath the surface of the sea, climbing into the sky on top of a 'ball of fire'. Llopis took pictures quickly [2, 3], changing position and checking his camera settings before continuing [4-7] (sequence continues overleaf).

4 ▶

UFOs From the Sea.
(continued). Antonio Llopis felt there was some connection between the strange pattern in the sky and the UFO that erupted from the sea—but he saw no readily visible link—neither one caused the other, they were just . . . simultaneous! Meteorologists later confirmed that sunset had been just over half an hour earlier, and if the sky-effect was caused by the setting sun, or by an aurora, it would be extremely unusual and like nothing they had heard of before.

Llopis took pictures for the duration of his sighting—about three minutes. The bright light from the object's 'tail' obliterated any details in the dark object itself. It accelerated rapidly—travelling 'through' the sky-pattern, according to Llopis—leaving behind a glowing trail and luminous cloud, which faded over half an hour [6, 7].

The event was witnessed by thousands of people, some of whom photographed it, providing evidence for an objective scientific assessment. Gilberto Naranjo, an engineer at a transmitting station on Mount Teide, said: "I thank God I have been allowed to witness this spectacle." He had his camera with him and took this photo [8].

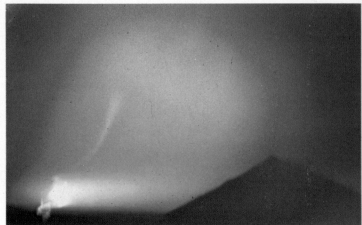
7

PSYCHIC PHENOMENA

Exorcism is one of the
universal functions of
priesthood, even in the
Church of England. Rev
Christopher Neil Smith, of
London, says he performs
about 500 exorcisms a year
– and here bids devils depart
from a possessed woman.

Possession. All over the world possession by gods or spirits is usually regarded as a cathartic ritual combining worship, purification and healing.

These snake-handlers belong to one of many radical traditional Christian communities in Tennessee [1]. The meetings begin with singing, clapping and dancing, punctuated by spirited preaching and shouted confessions. As trance comes they are possessed by the Holy Ghost, and believe a pure faith will protect them from the dangers of playing with deadly snakes, drinking strychnine and playing with fire (see p.118).

Similarly rhythmic drumming and dancing, and a state of mixed terror and excitement, in awe of the fearsome Voodoo gods, brings trance possession to these dancers in Haiti [2].

During the kris dance of Bali, the evil witch Rangda temporarily defeats a heroic beast, called Barong. At that moment dozens of Barong's frenzied helpers turn their kris-knives on themselves [3, 4]. Because of their trance there is little blood and wounds heal in hours.

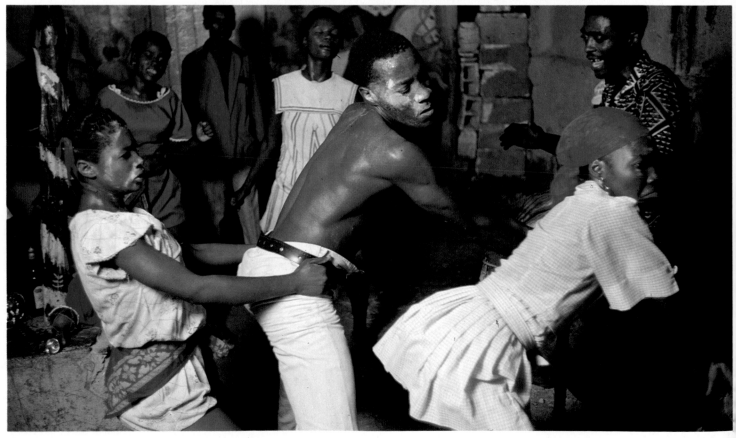

3, 4 ▶

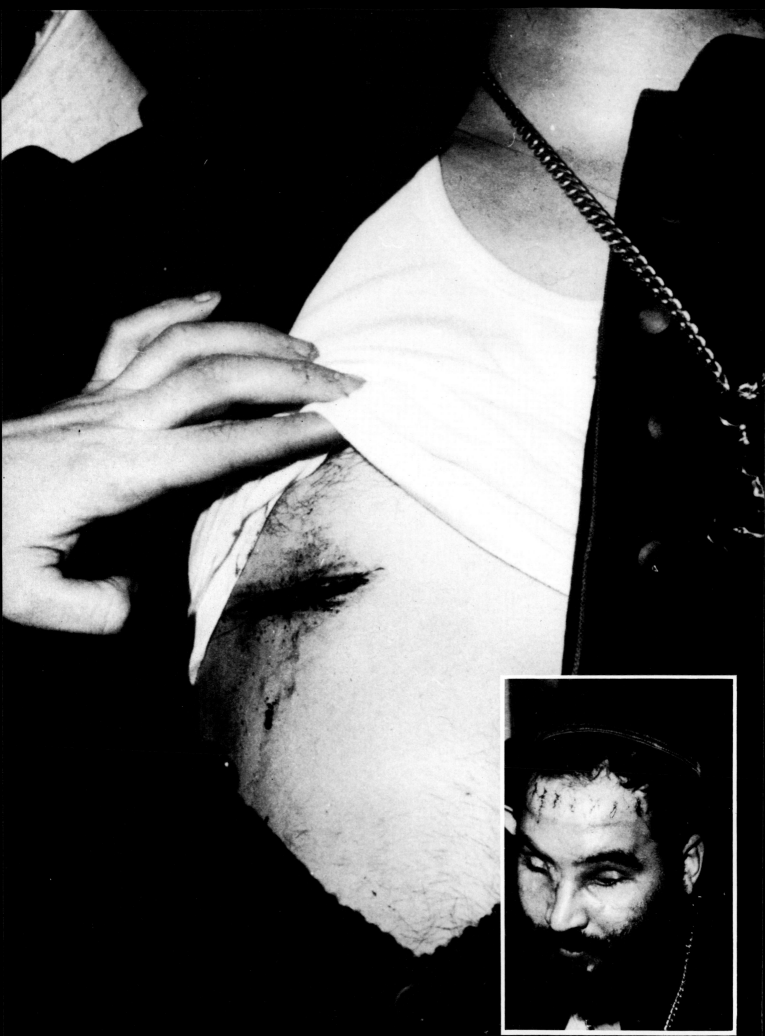

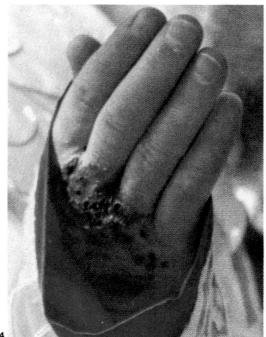

Stigmata.

Since the stigmatisation of St Francis of Assisi in 1224 – the first recorded case – there have been a few hundred people, mostly women, who have been marked with replicas of the wounds of Christ's crucifixion.

Clemente Dominguez, a Spanish visionary and self-proclaimed pope from Palmar de Troya, near Seville, regularly developed the chest wound [1] and the 'Crown of Thorns' [2, inset] during his public ecstasies in the late 1970s. He was quite the opposite to Padre Pio Forgione, who was a model of piety, humility and simplicity. Pio, who died in 1968, covered up his profusely bleeding wounds and appeared in public only to conduct Mass [3, 4]. Many medical examinations were made of Pio's wounds – his hands were pierced right through.

Up until Easter 1971 this form of stigmatisation was a strictly Catholic phenomenon, until nine-year-old Cloretta Robertson, an otherwise ordinary schoolgirl, of Oakland, California, became the first black non-Catholic stigmatic [5]. Several doctors observed, through a microscope, blood seeping through her skin in the localised patches. Her condition soon passed never to return.

Teresa Neumann was a classic stigmatic. From a poor German family, she worked at menial local jobs until mysterious illnesses confined her to the Bavarian village of Konnersreuth for the rest of her life. During the Lent of 1926, aged 28, she had a vision of the Passion of Christ. Thereafter, every Easter, the wounds appeared in her flesh, and she lost a lot of weight and blood. Under close medical scrutiny most of her life, she is said to have lived for years taking no sustenance except the wine and wafer during Mass. Her unique square-shaped wounds were still visible after her death in 1962 [6].

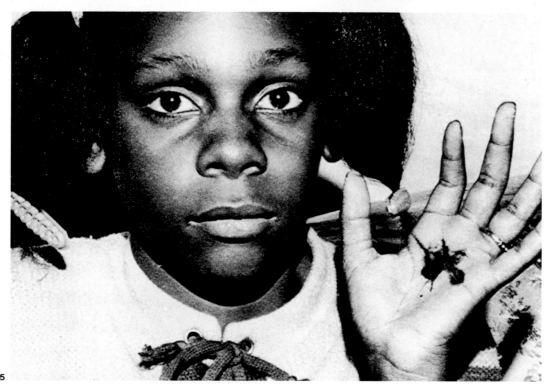

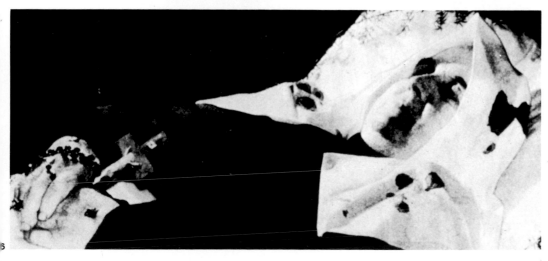

Bleeding Images. An authentic example of a popularly acclaimed miracle occurred at Syracuse, Sicily, in the autumn of 1953, when a poor family found their plastic image of 'The Immaculate Heart of Mary' shedding apparently genuine tears [1].

Less rare are portraits of Christ which ooze blood-like fluid, often from the traditional sites of the crucifixion wounds. One of the most celebrated incidents developed sporadically over ten years, from September 1911, when the priest of the French village of Mirebeau-en-Poitou, Abbé Vachere, found a small painting of Christ dripping blood [2, 3]. The phenomenon spread to a small statue, Hosts consecrated during Mass, and a replica of the first painting.

More recently we learned of this bleeding image from Roswell, New Mexico [4]. Kathy Mallot had bought, for her grandmother, Willie Mae Seymore, a fairly ordinary religious memento encased in plastic, at a drugstore. While visiting her grandmother in May 1979, they noticed blood pooling beneath the portrait's eye and falling to the bottom of the frame.

When her 26in (66cm) plaster statue of Christ began to bleed, in April 1975, so many people flocked to see it that Mrs Russell Poore, of Boothwyn, Pennsylvania, turned her front porch into a shrine [5]. When the statue was moved to St Luke's Episcopalian Church, Eddystone, near Philadelphia, the plaster hands were removed for examination and continued to ooze as the investigator held them.

The analysis of the substance seeping from the huge crucifix in the rural Brazilian village of Porto das Caixas [6], showed it was human blood. It first began to flow from the 300-year-old wooden crucifix in 1968, since when, it has been credited with at least eight miracle cures.

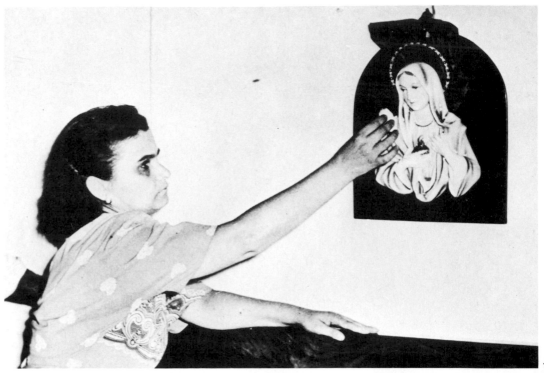

6►

Ectoplasm. Most séance phenomena involve the use of 'ectoplasm', a hypothetical and ethereal form of matter or energy projected by the medium's body. Normally invisible, it can be solidified into material objects or even animated bodies (see pp.106-109) which are best observed in red light.

Stanislawa P., a Polish medium, studied by Baron Schrenck von Notzing in 1913, produced ectoplasm consistently. A net over her face precludes the possibility of regurgitating concealed material [1].

Jack Webber, a medium operating in London in the 1930s, produced ribbons of ectoplasm with 'grippers' on the end [2]. There is some suggestion that ectoplasmic 'arms' are responsible for the movement and levitation of objects (see pp.126-129), and in the 1910s many experiments were carried out by Dr W.J. Crawford on the mediumistic girls of the Goligher family in Belfast. Here, an ectoplasmic lever from Kathleen Goligher, 18, about to lift a table [3], registers a load of 1lb (2.2 kg).

Thomas Lynn, a young miner from the north of England, satisfied many investigators during 1928-29 with authentic ectoplasmic structures appearing from his solar plexus. At the British College of Psychic Science, in March 1929, this luminous 'finger' played a zither [4].

In 1972 these remarkable pictures of an ectoplasm-like substance were taken at the University of California, Los Angeles. Under the watchful eyes of Dr Thelma Moss, Olga Worrall, one of America's most respected mediums, held a strip of film between the tips of her fingers, for about three minutes without touching the emulsion. Dr Moss then promptly placed it in a developing dish to reveal these curious patterns [5, 6].

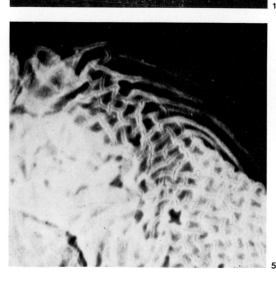

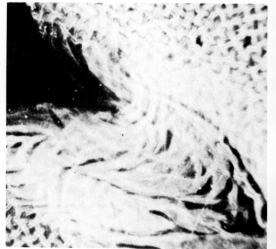

4 ►

PSYCHIC PHENOMENA

Mediumship. The range of phenomena manifested by Margery Crandon, a young wife from Boston, Massachusetts, was 'remarkable'.

It began in 1923, when Margery, then in her mid-20s, and her friends played with a Ouija board. It seemed to respond dramatically to her alone. Loud raps would be heard in the house during séances, and soon Margery was entering trances during which the alleged spirit of her dead brother, Walter, claimed credit for the phenomena. These included trance-writing in nine languages, including Chinese characters; levitating tables; disembodied voices and music; moving lights; clocks stopped at a distance at appointed times; and a variety of materializations.

Margery produced many kinds of ectoplasmic structure (see also pp.74-5), like this 'voice-box' which helped, it is said, in making the ghostly voices [1].

In 1924 Margery sat for a committee convened by *Scientific American* magazine. Among other tests she had Walter dip his invisible ectoplasm hand into melted wax to build up this phantom hand [2, 3]. But the committee could not agree on what it had seen and did not qualify the unsubstantiated charges of fraud made by its more vociferous members.

In other sessions for investigators in Europe, America and Britain, Margery produced a range of phenomena under test conditions. This photo shows dark ectoplasm exuding from her navel, while a sitter thoughtfully protects her modesty with a handkerchief [4]. Indeed there was a strong undercurrent of repressed sexuality and exhibitionism in her behaviour and phenomena, and she was even accused of concealing her props in her vagina. She was never really given a fair hearing, falling victim to the character assassination of men out to prove all spiritualism was bunkum.

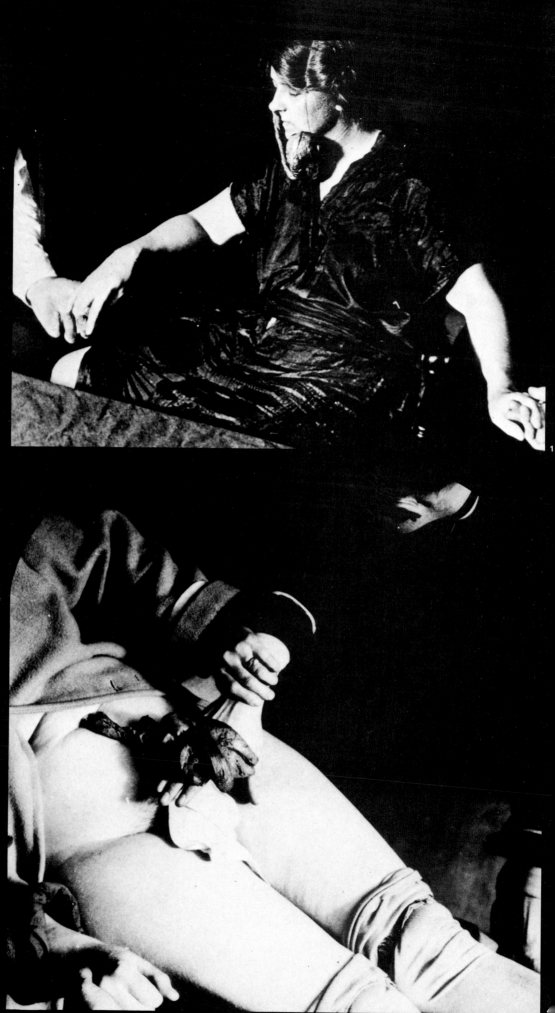

she bought an Instamatic camera and immediately noticed strange streaks of light, misty swirls, and even phantom figures in her photos (see pp.101-102). Gladys, a vivacious East London housewife, who up until then concerned herself with healing work, was told, through sittings with other mediums, that she was being trained for other kinds of work.

Anyone who has tried to take a photo in near darkness without a flash will know the result is usually a very under exposed print. Yet Gladys works in virtual darkness, using a very dim red light, with her simple Instamatic camera on a tripod, and holds a cable release. A typical photo [1] shows a mysterious white monkey on her lap. The photos seem impossible – but they exist, Gladys believes, because her spirits provide the light.

With no other source of light in her sanctuary, a stream of light – ectoplasm? – pours from Gladys' chest, reflecting on the surfaces of the metal trumpet and the table it rests on [2]. Then Gladys seems to be de-materializing while the trumpet appears in two places at once [3]. Gladys told us she is unable to move during these events and certainly did not get up or reach for the trumpet.

This de-materializing effect recurs in many of the photos. One taken in daylight under normal shutter conditions should have shown her solidly in her chair [4]. At the end of 1974, a disbelieving local photographer called with an infra-red film and reluctantly agreed to take the shots in the near-darkness. One of these [5] shows a phantom hand touching Gladys' camera, while one of the sitters, in the chair to the left, seems to be fading away. Then, most astonishing of all, on six of the 36 frames on the roll, Gladys' camera and tripod have completely vanished [6].

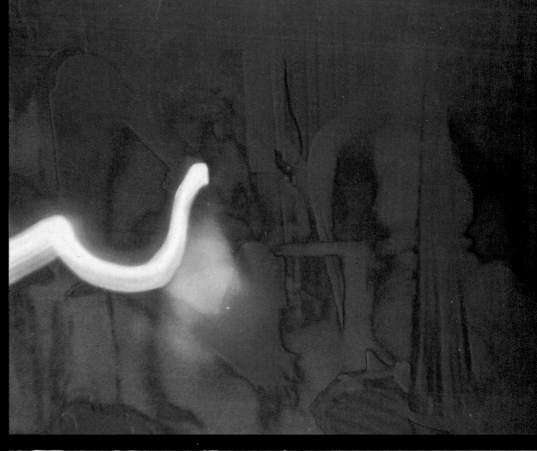

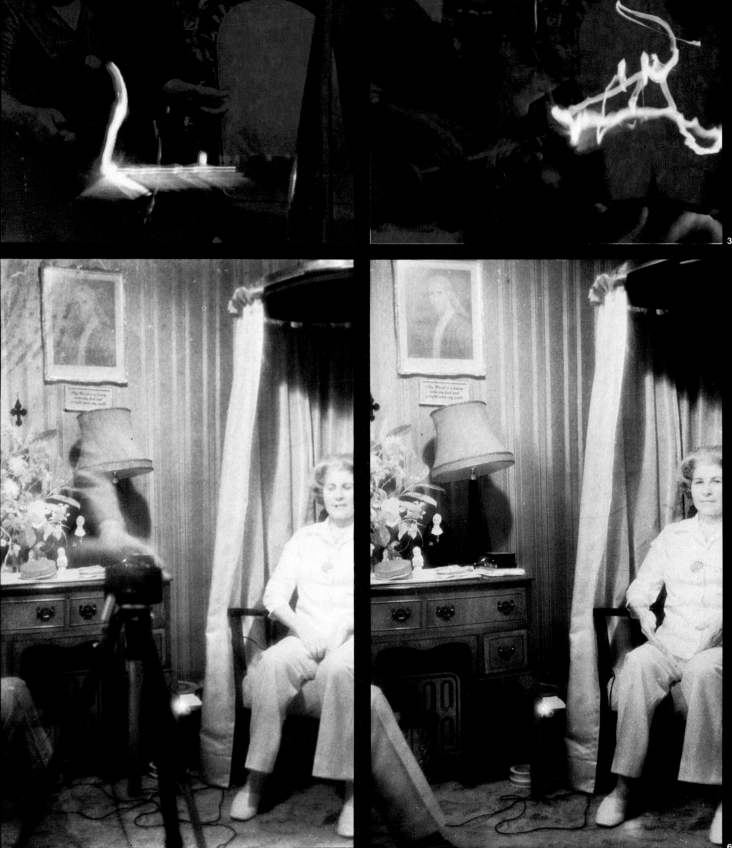

Thoughtography. Ted Serios, self-described as an ''unemployed Chicago bellhop'', came to the notice of Dr Jule Eisenbud early in 1964. Serios had an ability he would demonstrate to anyone who took an interest – he could project mental images onto photographic film, sometimes with the lens cap still on, and sometimes with no lens at all on the camera. His talent was unpredictable and seemed to depend on Serios working himself up, then glaring at the camera through a small cardboard tube he called his 'gismo' (see title pages). The 'gismos' were constantly examined by investigators and never contained anything suspicious. Dr Eisenbud was intrigued enough to spend more than a year studying Ted and his results.

On one occasion Ted produced this image [1], identified as an old livery-stable in Chicago which was located a few days later and photographed with Ted posing outside [2]. In Ted's picture the window and door are elongated and appear bricked up; the texture of the wall differs from that of the real building; and attempts to trace a wall-poster that matched the one to the left of the door failed. Eisenbud concluded that Ted had not photographed the real building, but somehow obtained an image that contained distorted elements from his memory or imagination.

There was no way to identify the origin of some of Ted's photos – like this shot apparently showing a Russian Vostok spacecraft [3] – while others clearly seem to be images seen in magazines, or films, etc., filtered through Ted's mind. The Royal Canadian Mounted Police identified this photo [4] as one of their Air Division hangars [5], but Ted had left his mark in the mis-spelling of 'Cainadian'.

Once, trying to picture the Hilton hotel at Denver, Colorado, Ted obtained this image of the Chicago Hilton instead [6].

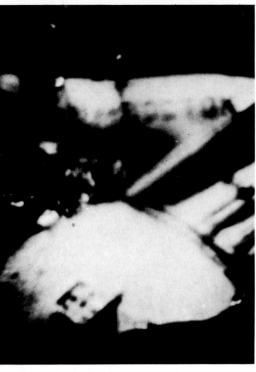

Thoughtography. For several years, Dr Berthold Schwarz, a practising psychiatrist with a keen interest in UFO phenomena, closely studied Mrs Stella Lansing, a Massachusetts housewife, whose psychic abilities unfolded after a series of UFO sightings and a close encounter. Stella was often impelled to start filming by chills or hunches, and produced over 500 regular 8 and Super 8 colour ciné films, with many frames on each reel revealing phantom faces, geometrically arranged marks and other curious effects, including artifacts which look like classic UFOs.

In 1973 Stella visited her employer, Mr C. and his family, and while there filmed two shows from the TV screen. When the cassette returned from developing she was shocked to find super-imposed faces, mirage-like effects on outdoor scenes, and this bizarre image which she interprets as a 'monk' in death-agony holding a flute-like rod [1]. Tucked into the margin of a frame of Mrs C.'s curtains was another bearded cowled face [2].

On other occasions Stella has found a bright clock-like pattern superimposed across the frames of whatever she was filming — here an overhead plane [3, inset top] — the enlarged details of which have resembled 'flying saucer' shapes [4, inset bottom] and BVM-type light flashes (see pp.92-3).

2

1, 3, 4 ▶

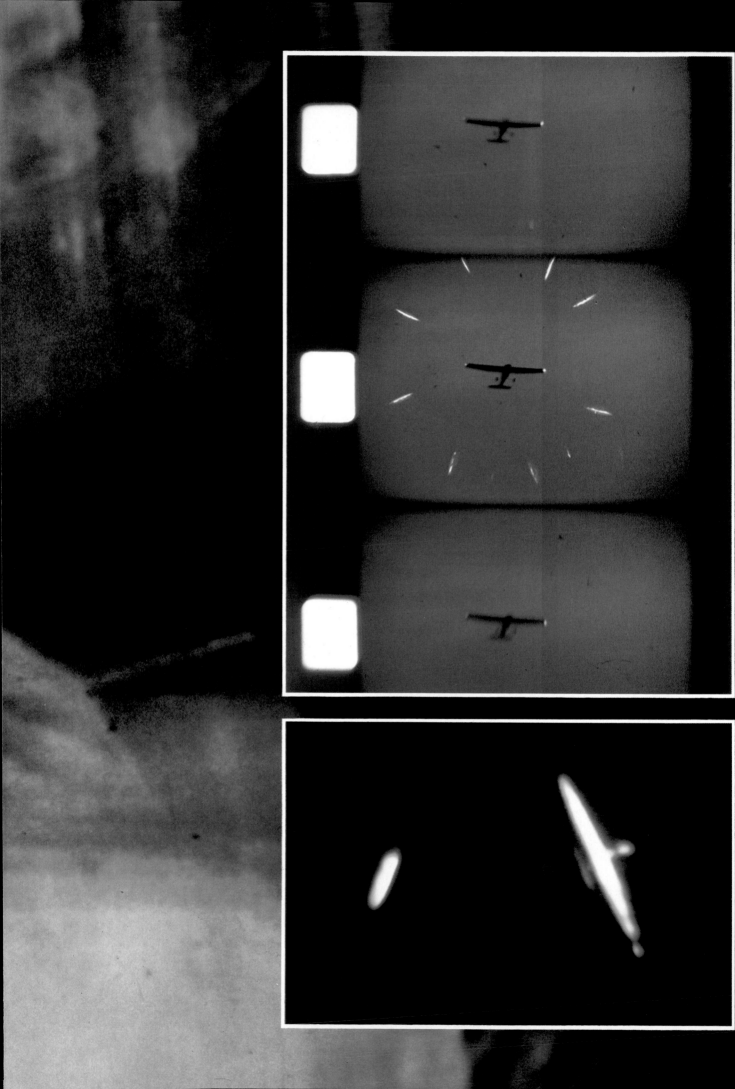

Thoughtography. During his study of Ted Serios, Dr Jule Eisenbud learned of the effects produced by brothers Richard and Fred Veilleux and their families, of Waterville, Maine. The brothers began experiments with a Ouija board in 1966 through which they received instructions about when and where to take pictures.

Among their first paranormal effects was this photo of Carol, Fred's daughter, in Pine Grove cemetery, in June 1968 [1], showing her surrounded by inexplicable fogging.

In April 1970, the Ouija board told the brothers to focus upon the east wall of the smallest room in their father's apartment – the result was this strange scene of a chariot [2]. At the same sitting Biblical quotations were given which related to the chariot.

This phantom face [3] appeared after the brothers were told, in June 1968, to point the camera at the east wall of Fred's kitchen and wait two minutes before taking the picture. They could not identify the portrait until two years later when they visited Denver, Colorado, while working with Dr Eisenbud. They found a copy of a historical magazine, *The West,* which contained an almost identical face, that of a long dead sheriff named Scott White [4].

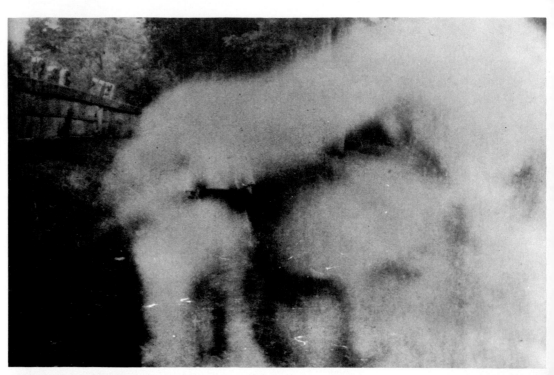

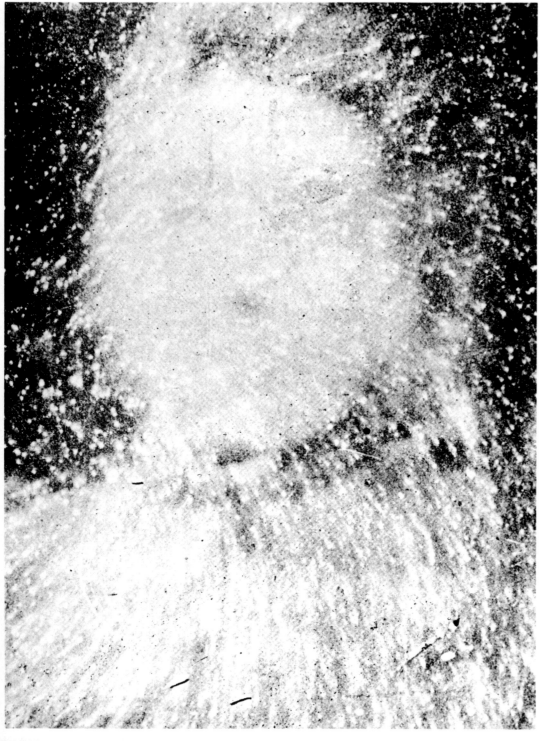

Thoughtography. Throughout the history of psychic photography there have been many attempts to photograph the human aura – a hypothetical field of energy which extends beyond the physical body forming a luminous envelope. Like the recent development of Kirlian photography (see pp.86-89) it was hoped that this would lead to a useful diagnostic tool, since the aura's size, shape and colour depended on the physical condition. Interestingly, it was also claimed that the aura responded to mental control and could be moulded and extended achieving effects at a distance from the body. This is one possible mechanism for thoughtography – psychokinesis (see pp.124-129) is another. This photograph of the aura of a young girl [5] from the work of Charles Lancelin at the turn of the century shows swirling feathery patterns which have been noticed in the results of Ted Serios (see p.80) and a Japanese psychic [6].

Professor Tomokichi Fukurai, of the Imperial University, Tokyo, was a leading Japanese psychic researcher who tested many psychics between 1910 and 1913. One of his subjects, a female with a secondary personality called 'The Goblin', could mentally imprint calligraphic characters onto plates sealed in lightproof wrappings. One of these [6] bears the feathery swirl mentioned above. Another of Fukurai's mediums developed a remarkable control and could project two halves of a character onto different plates which would then match up [7].

7

85

PSYCHIC PHENOMENA

Kirlian Photography. In 1949, a Soviet couple, Semyon and Valentina Kirlian, patented a camera-less method of photography. Objects placed directly onto the film within a high frequency electrical field are surrounded by bright discharges – like this image of a fresh orange [1] – which some believe could be the life-force itself made visible. One Kirlian researcher, Harry Oldfield, took the growing core from the centre of an onion, and photos taken at intervals show it becoming less vibrant as it died [2-4].

It is claimed that Kirlian photography shows up the differences between health-giving and junk foods. Similarly, it seems the vital nourishing energy of vegetables is diminished by cooking. Compare fresh cabbage [5] with the visually lifeless appearance of the same piece after pressure cooking [6].

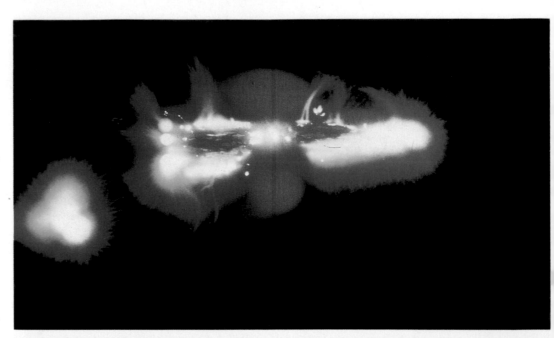

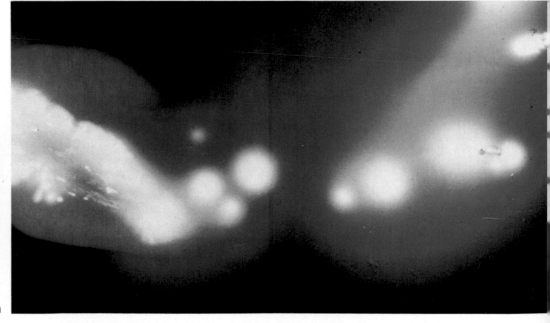

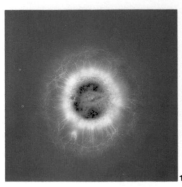

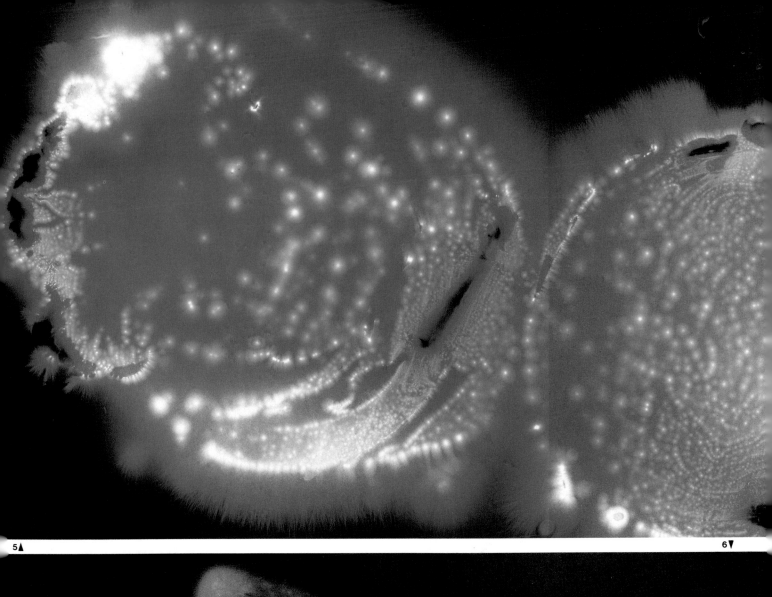

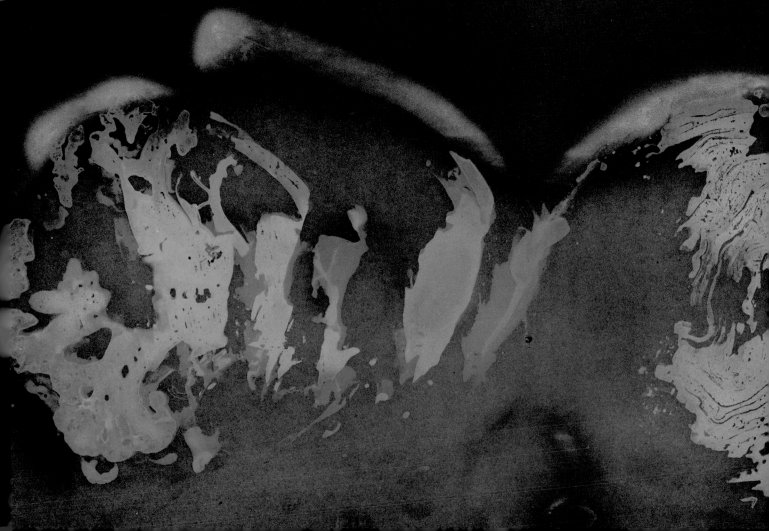

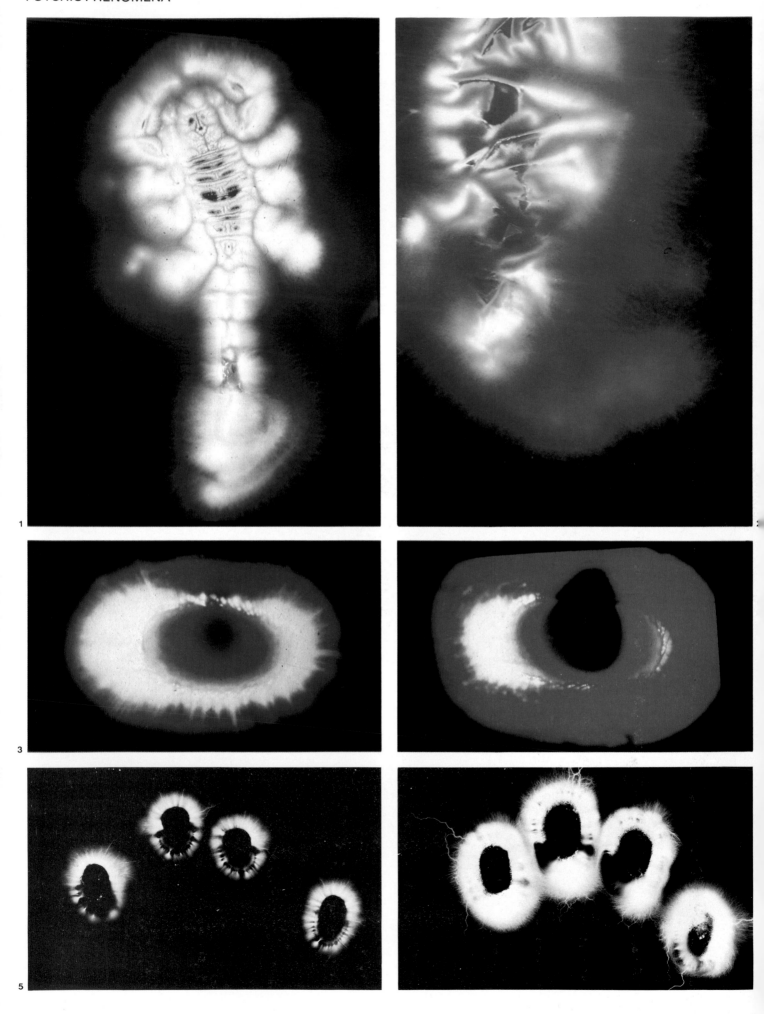

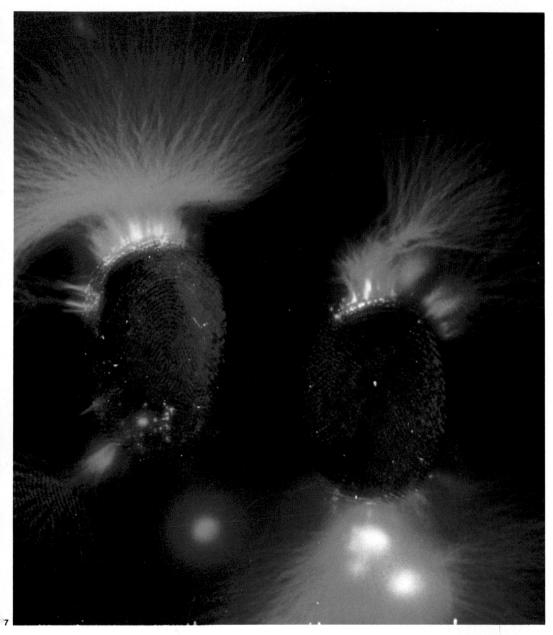

Kirlian Photography. Inside the high-frequency field of the Kirlian 'camera' all objects become surrounded by an aura – like this scorpion [1], or these cheek-cells from a child's mouth [2] – and many researchers claim that the size, shape and colour of this aura is a powerful diagnostic tool. Kirlian images have successfully identified different drugs, and even diseases like cancer.

The process can record quite subtle changes in the plant, animal or human being. These photos show a fingertip during pregnancy [3] and at the on-set of labour [4]. Similarly, these fingertips are of a girl before [5] and after [6] prayer. The medium Matthew Manning has several times demonstrated an ability to control the extent of the discharges from his fingertips [7], reinforcing the idea that the images reflect some part of the human energy field.

Among the startling experiments with Kirlian effects is one by researcher Harry Oldfield on two samples of rock from a roadside wall in Ireland: compare one from the reputedly haunted site of a fatal coaching accident [8], with the other sample taken further along the road [9].

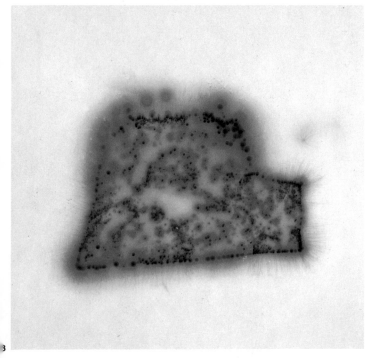

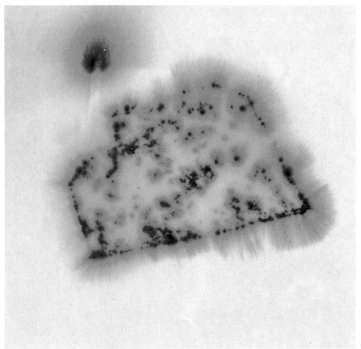

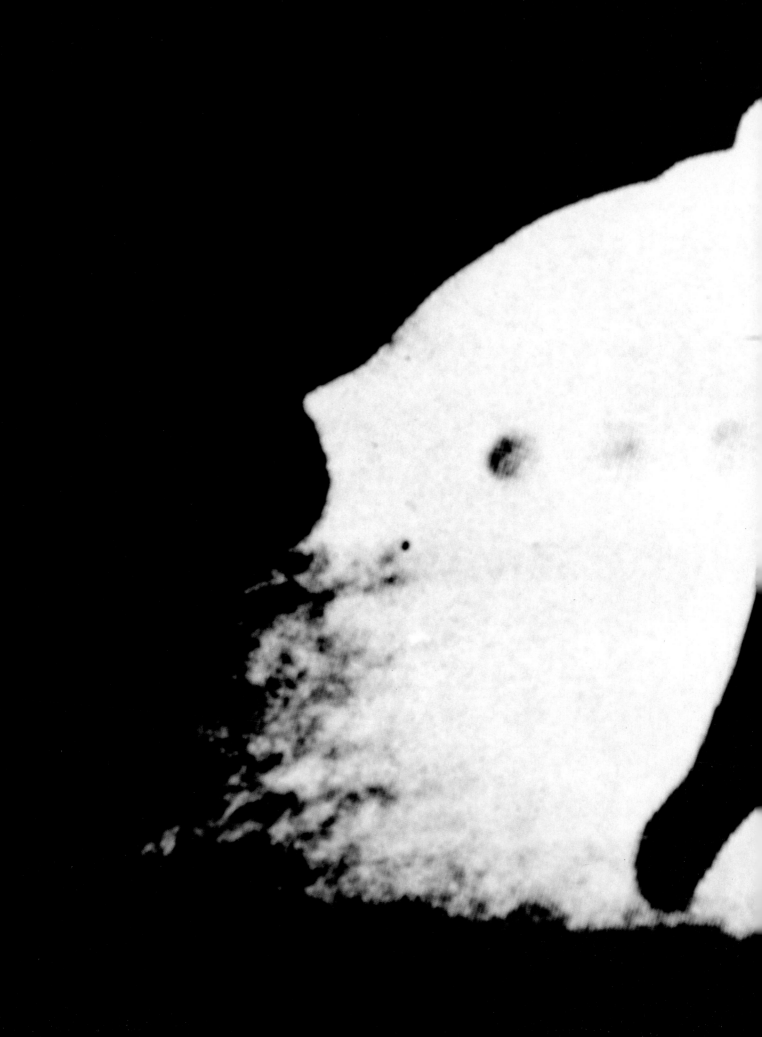

PARANORMAL PERSONS

In the 1950s, Howard Menger, claimed he had a startling series of meetings with people from other planets, and even had a guided tour of the solar system in a UFO. Not wishing to be recognized, one Venusian only agreed to be photographed in silhouette against his glowing craft.

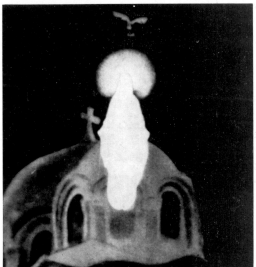

BVM and Angels. In April 1968, crowds gathered outside the Egyptian church of St Mary at Zeitoun, Cairo, saw glowing forms of white doves and the Blessed Virgin Mary (BVM), gliding along the church roof [1,2].

This photo [3] was taken at San Damiano, Italy, the scene of BVM apparitions to visionary Rosa Quattrini since 1964. Is it a figure of the Virgin Mary as many believe? An almost identical shape was snapped un-awares by Judith Luckwell at Easter 1977 when a voice told her to photograph a flower cross on the beach at Pass-a-grille, Florida [4].

After his researches with Stella Lansing (see p.82) Dr Berthold Schwarz observed strange images developing in his own films. This dramatic BVM image appeared when he filmed two microwave towers at Green Pond, New Jersey [5].

Veronica Leuken, a New York housewife, has had regular visions since 1968. During her public vigils in Flushing Meadow Park many 'miraculous photos' have been taken – like this one [6] – in November 1978, apparently showing the BVM in the sky, a pointing arm on the left and cryptic symbols. Another photo shows Veronica in ecstasy, obliterated by strange lights, as, she claims, the Virgin placed the infant Jesus into her arms [7].

PARANORMAL PERSONS

Portraits of Christ. For well over 60 years, a picture, said to show Jesus against a snowy scene, has been popping up in the British press [1]. The earliest version we know of [2] is said to have been taken on 15 July 1920 by Mildred Swanson of Seattle, Washington, when her camera shutter released itself, according to a note on the back of a copy sent to Sir Arthur Conan Doyle in 1926.

The strangest picture of Christ must be one originating from Father Pellegrino Ernetti, a monk and distinguished professor of music, teaching in Rome and Venice. He claims to have invented a 'time camera' which turns ancient sounds into visual images, and with it, claims to have photographed the whole life of Jesus, including the climax on Calvary [3].

This famous photograph [4] resulted when an American bomber crewman wanted to photograph his companion planes during a mission over Korea. This face of Christ in the clouds appeared after he had sent the film back to his parents in Chicago for development.

Like the photos above [1, 2] we know tantalizingly little about our next two, and yet what we do know conflicts. Versions of this image of a robed figure in the sky [5] believed by many to be a genuine photo of Jesus, have come from Illinois, Texas, Virginia and New York. Our own copy came from Canada, where it was being circulated by nuns. The second figure-in-the-sky photo [6], came to us from the Mary Help of Mothers Shrine, in Bayside, New York.

Finally, portraits of Jesus, turn up as simulacra – spontaneous images on unlikely surfaces. In this case Maria Rubio, of Lake Arthur, New Mexico, was frying tortillas, in October 1977, when she was astonished to see one marked with a vague face-like formation [7]. Now the tortilla is enshrined at a local church where it is visited by thousands who believe it is an authentic image of Christ.

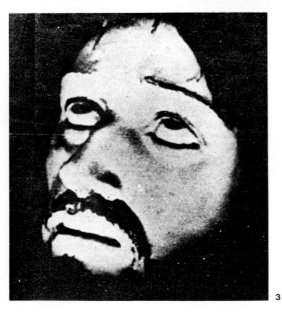

3

6

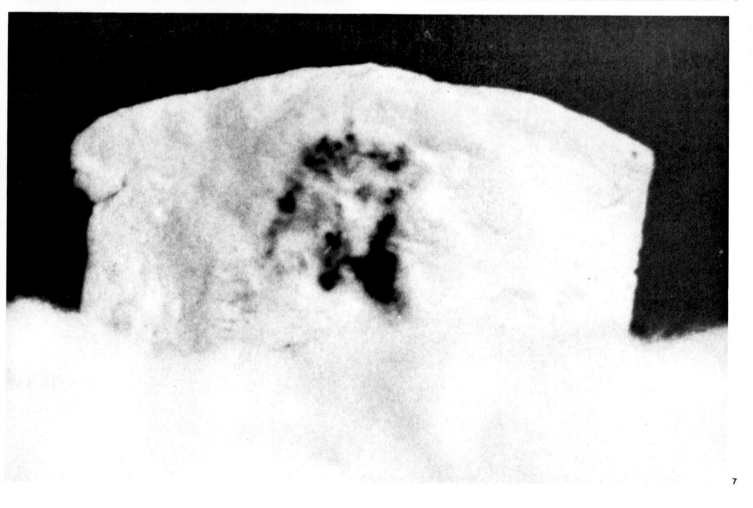

7

PARANORMAL PERSONS

Aliens. Since the first UFO scares of the 1940s rumours have abounded of crashed UFOs (see p.44:1) and their dead occupants allegedly preserved in government establishments. Not much is known about this photograph [1], said to show the body of a dead pilot of a UFO which came down near Mexico City in the 1950s. The body was believed to have been sent for examination in Germany, but that was the last anyone heard of it.

James Templeton, of Carlisle, Cumbria, took a photograph of his daughter Elizabeth, 5, on the remote banks of the Solway Firth in May 1966. Templeton was sure there had been no-one else around, but there was no mistaking the strange figure in the photo [2]. Across the Solway Firth lay the Chapel Cross nuclear plant so it was inevitably suggested that one of the nuclear workers, in protective suit, was trying to frighten off the Templetons. But the phantom in the 'spacesuit' soon came to the attention of the UFO research community, who suggested that UFO beings were invisible to the eye but not to the camera.

During the extensive 1973 UFO 'flap' in the USA, an Alabama police chief, Jeff Greenhaw, investigated a report of a landed UFO in a rural area near Falkville. He suddenly saw the form of a silver-suited humanoid coming towards him out of the night, and managed to shoot four Polaroid photos [3]. He chased the creature in his car but it vanished.

Like so many of our photographers in this book, Giichi Shiota, a professional photographer of Kawanoe City, Japan, was prompted by a hunch to wait late at night with his camera, on a deserted plot in the city. Suddenly he saw what looked like a "spaceman" who appeared to break into independent images enveloped in strangely coloured "electrical discharges" [4-6].

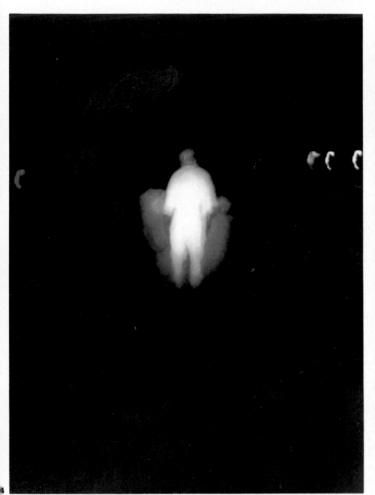
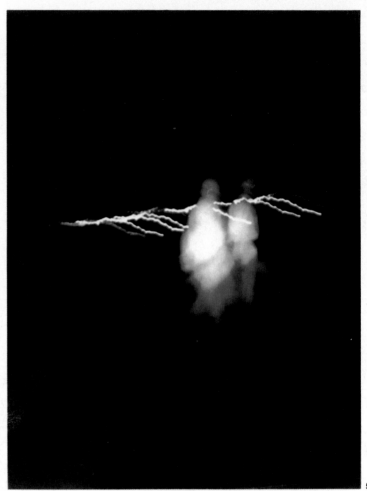

5

6

Phantoms. When phantom images appear in photographs of churches, the misty forms are inevitably interpreted as the ghosts of priests. Gordon Carroll, a keen young photographer, set up his equipment inside the Norman church of St Mary's, at Woodford, Northamptonshire, in June 1966, to record its architecture. He was surprised to find he had also caught a figure kneeling at the altar [1]. A similar 'kneeling priest' appeared on a photo of the ornate altar of St Nicholas's church, at Arundel, Sussex, taken by a reputable local solicitor in 1940 [2].

When Lady Palmer visited the Basilica at Domrémy, France, in June 1925, recently dedicated to St Joan of Arc, her companion, a Miss Townsend, took this portrait of her alone inside, which later revealed the phantom forms of two priests, apparently in archaic dress [3].

The vicar of Newby church, in north Yorkshire, Rev K.F. Lord, found this bizarre apparition, on his own photo of the church's altar, in the early 1960s [4].

4

PARANORMAL PERSONS

Phantoms. Many 'ghosts' appear in domestic scenes. This headless dog was an invisible visitor to the garden of Arthur Springer in 1916 [1]. Springer, a retired police inspector, of Tingewick, Buckinghamshire, is certain there was no dog in sight when the photo was taken.

Sybil Corbet wanted a souvenir of her stay at the Cheshire country house of Lord Combermere, in December 1891, and set up her camera and tripod in the fine panelled library. She developed the plate herself and was astonished to find the form of an old man on the left [2], later identified as Lord C. himself in his favourite chair. Coincidentally, Lord C. was being buried at the very time the photo was taken.

Mrs Mabel Chinnery, of Ipswich, Suffolk, visited her mother's grave on 22 March 1959, to take a few photographs, and used up the film snapping her husband alone in the car – or so she thought. A friend seeing the photos later pointed out the image of Mrs Chinnery's mother sitting in the back seat, to the Chinnery's astonishment [3]. A strikingly similar photograph was taken in March 1979, by London medium Gladys Hayter of her daughter Dawn, who had just driven up in her car. Dawn was alone, but the photo shows the image of an unknown blonde-headed girl in the back seat [4].

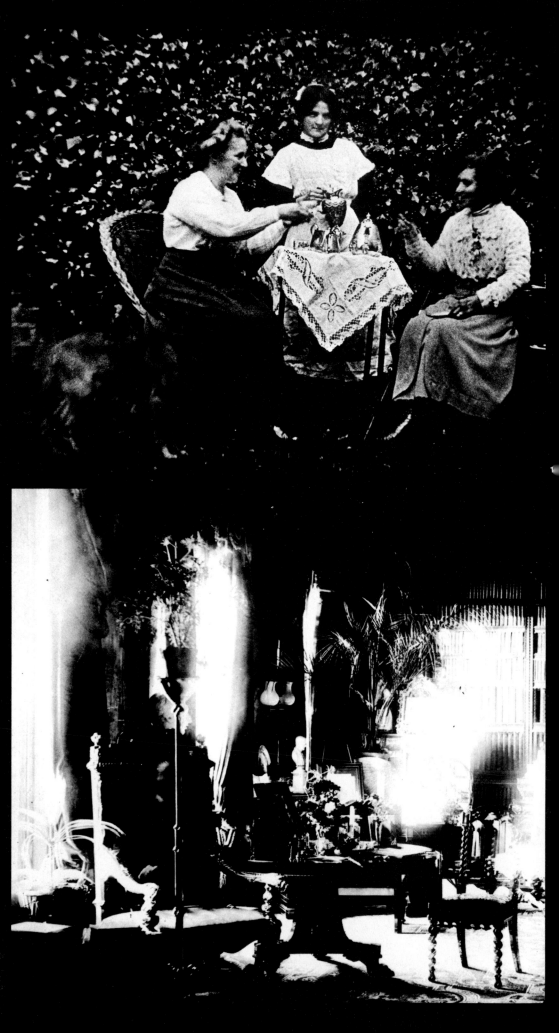

3

4

PARANORMAL PERSONS

Phantoms. Gladys Hayter, a London medium, was always aware of the presence of her spirit helpers. She took this picture herself in 1972. It should have shown clearly a friend and healer, Stephen Webb, ministering to a patient in Gladys's sanctuary [1]. After development, the two were found to be almost obliterated by cloudy lights with two shadowy forms of 'spirit doctors' behind and between them.

During a trip to Australia in 1959, Rev R.S. Blance went to Corroboree Rock, a well known aboriginal ritual site near Alice Springs. To his surprise he found he had also caught a strangely garbed figure to the right of the clearing [2].

George and Nancy Clamp, of Coalville, Leicestershire visited Mount St. Bernard Abbey, and took a few shots of the grounds with their Instamatic camera. In one view, of a Virgin Mary statue atop a rockery, appeared a cloudy form [3], which has been variously attributed to a dead friar, a ghost, or an appearance of the BVM herself (see p.92).

One of the most thoroughly documented photos of a ghost was taken in November 1971, when a group of responsible students from Bucks Community College, Newtown, Pennsylvania, spent weeks investigating an ancient haunted house in nearby Levittown, including a survey of the whole house using colour infra-red film — out of 120 slides, five proved unusual, and one of these [4] seems to show a "non-solid, non-heat producing human-shaped form." The blue colouring indicates electro-magnetic emissions.

3

4

Phantoms. In the early days of spirit photography ethereal faces and figures appeared indiscriminately, but one face peers out at us more frequently than others – Sir Arthur Conan Doyle. Because of his enthusiastic espousal of spiritualism later in his life, this lady, among many others, obviously thought Conan Doyle's appearance would be an endorsement from beyond the grave [1].

Other photographers would hoax their sitters with pre-exposed plates, claiming the figures were deceased relatives. This girl's phantom playmate may be genuine – but it is doubtful [2].

A series of ghostly faces were obtained in colour by American medium John Myers, with an Instamatic camera. The photos were taken against the background of the crypt where lie the ashes of Marilyn Monroe [3]. Certainly the face resembles Marilyn's, but our suspicions were aroused about their authenticity when we noticed that the configuration of the 'ectoplasm' cloud and the scale of the 'extra' in relation to the camera was identical in all the photos.

Whereas other photos on this spread are likely to be fakes, we accept that the phenomenon does genuinely occur, sometimes under test conditions, but usually when least expected, as some of our other examples show. When college student Wendy Sternberg, of Buffalo, New York, needed a photo for her identity card in 1974, she discovered a spontaneous profile of an old man or woman behind her [4] where there was nothing but the flat wall of the photo-booth.

PARANORMAL PERSONS

Materializations. Full materializations are less common today than in the heyday of spiritualism at the turn of the century. In 1953, a spiritualist's summer camp was held at Ephrata, Pennsylvania, and, before a large audience, medium Ethel Post Parrish materialized her spirit guide, 'Silver Belle', from wreaths of ectoplasm [1-6]. Silver Belle, looking very much like an idealized Indian princess, was photographed at nearly one minute intervals in infra-red light, and for half an hour sported with the audience, some of whom touched her.

Sir Oliver Lodge's interest in spiritualism became public knowledge on the publication of his book, *Raymond,* in which he described how he received proofs of the survival of his son, Raymond, who was killed in the first World War. In October 1929, Raymond's face appeared in a stream of ectoplasm from a medium's nostril [7] – here with his service photo for comparison [8]. The photograph was taken by Dr T. Glen Hamilton, of Winnipeg, a Canadian physician widely respected for his 15 years of photographing mediums under test conditions.

In 1920, Franek Kluski, aged 46, sat for some famous pioneer psychic researchers in Paris. 'Kluski' was a pseudonym – in daily life he was a respectable Polish intellectual who had conversed with phantoms since childhood, not realizing that others did not see as he did. His speciality was the materialization of animal forms, from large hawk-like creatures [9], to a shambling smelly ape-like-man [10], who occasionally rearranged the furniture with great ease, and one day lifted one of the sitters into the air.

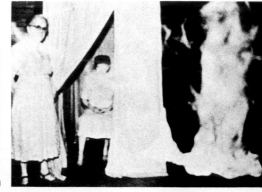

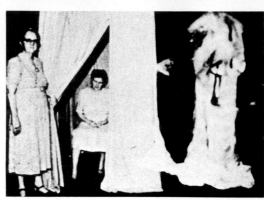

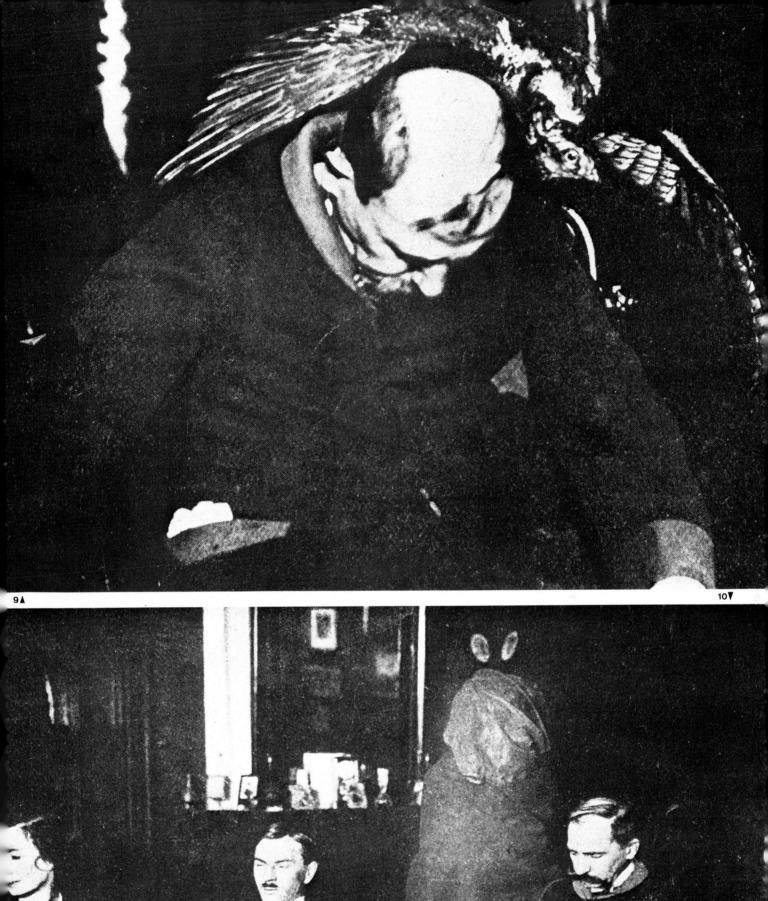

PARANORMAL PERSONS

Materializations. A number of mediums have claimed to have materialized the spirit of a girl called Katie King, but none match the dramatic appearances of Katie in the séances of a teenage Londoner called Florence Cook. Accounts of these, the first full-bodied materializations to an English medium, were hardly taken seriously before the investigations of the great physicist, Sir William Crookes. He won Florence's trust by inviting her to stay with his family occasionally, resulting in a series of photographs by Crookes himself, of which only a few survived.

Florence was often found collapsed by her chair [1] while the ectoplasmic form of Katie King posed for the camera with Crookes [2], mingled with the sitters [3], and on her own [4].

Opponents of spiritualism ridiculed Crookes – suggesting he had either been fooled by a buxom girl, or connived in fraud to cover an affair with her – pointing out the similarity between Katie and Florence herself [5]. Crookes replied that there were many differences between the two girls: Florence had her ears pierced and Katie did not; Katie's complexion was fair and her neck smooth where Florence's was dark and her neck rough; and Katie's fingers were longer than Florence's.

The matter was clinched, for Crookes at least, when on 29 March 1874, he had the opportunity to see both girls together.

1

2

5

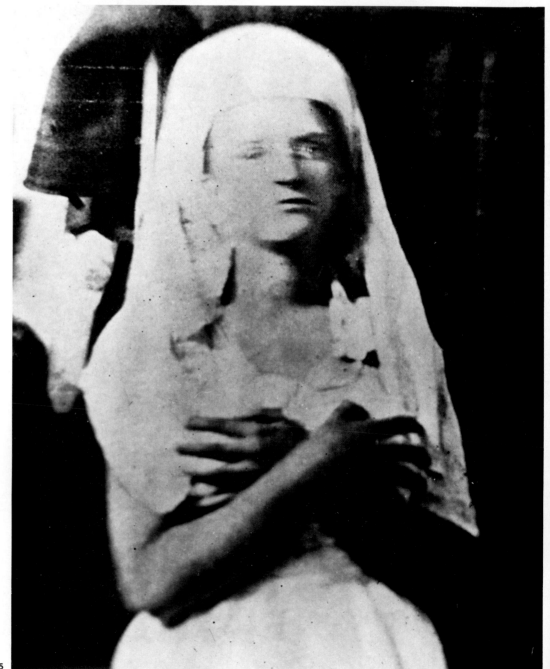

4 ▶

MIND OVER MATTER

In 1909 a young Polish medium, Stanislawa Tomczyk, held a plastic ball in mid-air by her 'psychic power'. Today this mysterious mind-over-matter force is called psychokinesis, or PK, and studied seriously in paraphysical laboratories.

Yoga. By a lifetime of meditation and practice the breath and the pulse-rate can be slowed down to a virtual state of suspended animation. In Lahore, in 1838, one man was buried alive in a padlocked box at the bottom of a pit filled in with earth, for 30 days, his grave guarded continuously by British soldiers. He was no mystic but a fakir who made a living as a magician — nevertheless the feat was an authentic performance of control over the mind, body and breath. A similar test was successfully endured by Egyptian fakir, Rahman Bey [1] who was buried alive at Carshalton, Surrey, in July 1938, before a panel of British doctors, scientists and sceptics.

Despite the continuing revelations from modern medical studies on yogis in laboratory conditions — here a doctor from the Menninger Foundation, Kansas, monitors the electrical activity in the brain of a yogi meditating on a bed of nails [2] — the mind-body relationship still retains most of its secrets. Curiously some westerners are able to duplicate these feats genuinely, often without the aid of an obvious trance, suggesting that mind-over-body control may be more universal than we think. Dutchman Mirin Dajo appears to conquer pain to order, and in his nightclub act regularly has thin rapiers thrust through his chest and abdomen without pain or infection [3].

Some feats are simply inexplicable. All we are able to tell you about this photo [4], is that the man, known as Amal Fakir, claims that a swallowed cord can be retrieved through his skin by an assistant who makes a small cut to extract it. Logic suggests a trick — there is no physiological basis for a passage between the stomach and the skin of the abdomen — yet the photo appears genuine. Could this be a form of apport?

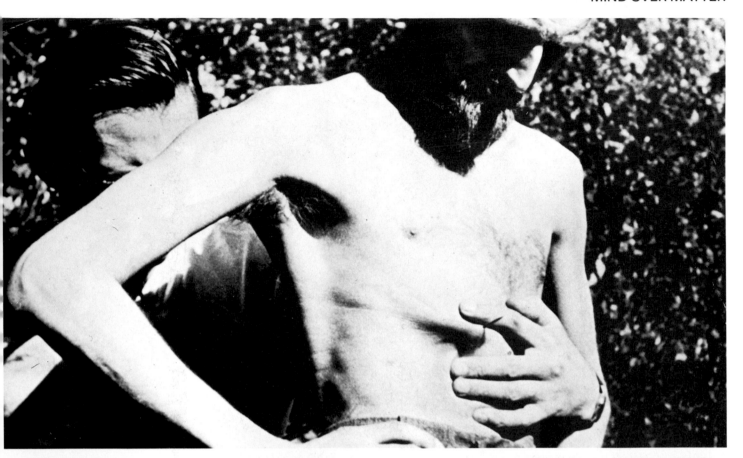

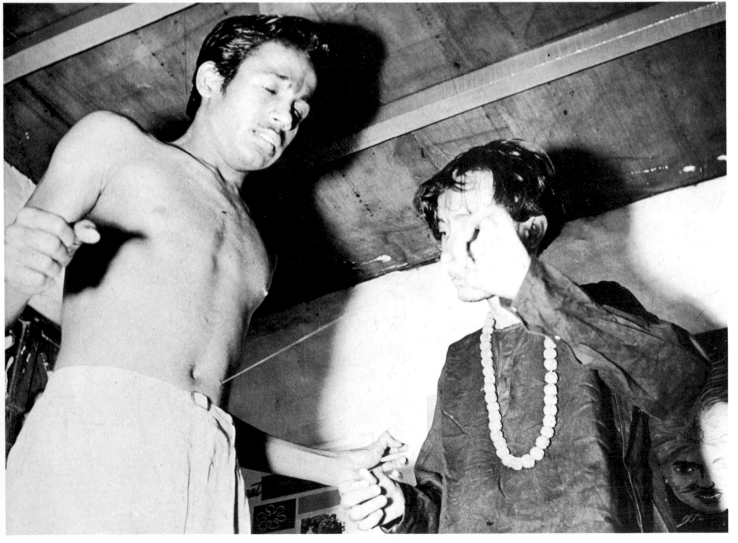

MIND OVER MATTER

Pain Immunity. There are some people with peculiarities of the nervous system which allow them to overrule, or not to feel, pain in some parts of their bodies like Paul Schollkopf [1] – and some of them, make a living from their debility.

Conversely, among otherwise ordinary people, pain immunity – like fire immunity (see p.118) – comes only in trance or ecstasy. This immunity can be conferred by priests or shamans, by fervent chants or prayers, or by ecstatic dancing.

At the Kataragama temple in Sri Lanka a ten-day festival is held each mid-year in honour of the god Skanda and his wives and retinue, at which devotees redeem the pledges made to them for luck and favours. People from all walks of life honour their part of the bargain by performing extraordinary austerities and self-mutilation, trusting completely to the god to protect them from harm and pain. Some roll around the temple complex; some walk on clogs studded with upwardly pointing nails; some walk over hot coals (see p.120); while a few thrust fearsome knives through their flesh [2].

The most extreme ritual consists of securing hooks through the strong muscles of the back, buttocks and thighs [3] and suspension from a wheeled frame [4]. In their ecstasy the devotees become possessed by the deities, and for several hours the bizarre mobile is trundled around bestowing blessings upon the crowds.

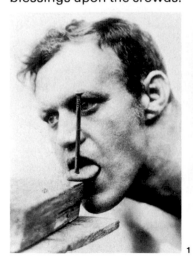

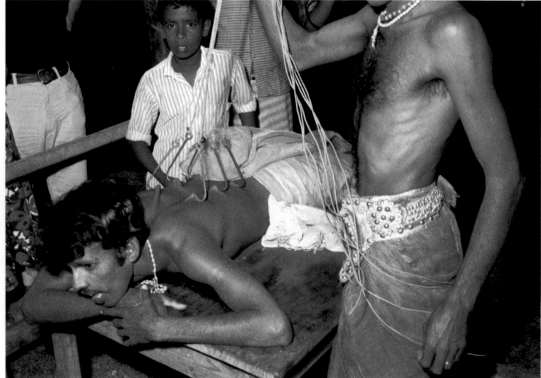

4 ▶

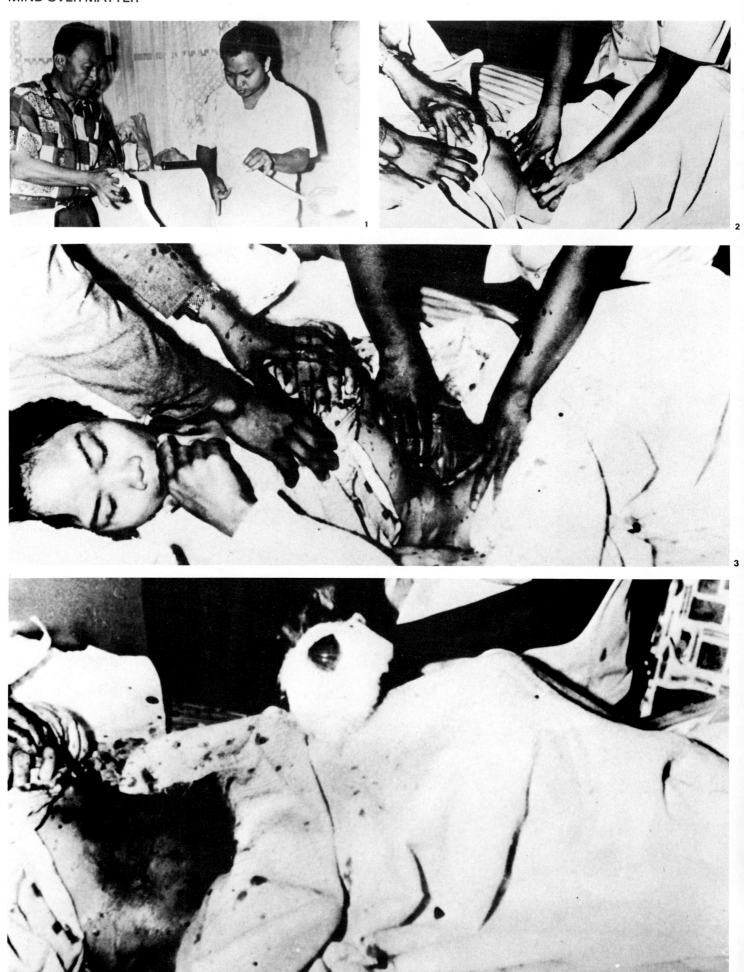

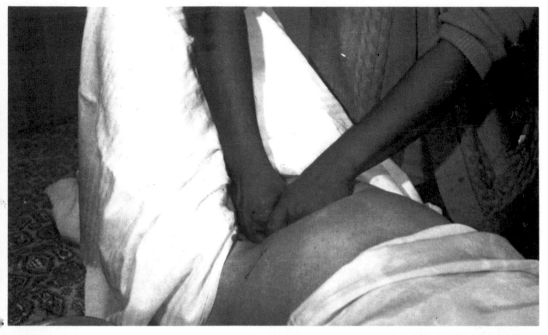

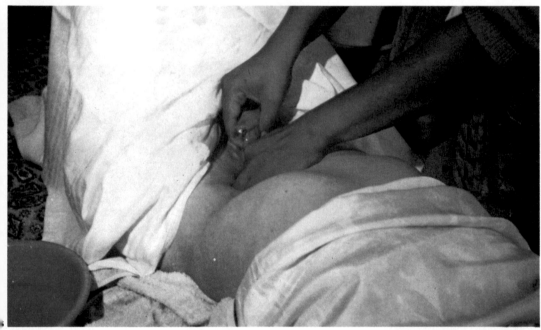

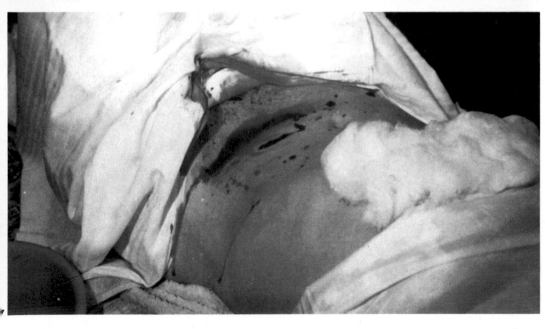

Psychic Surgery. There are two kinds of psychic surgeon: those who mime operations on the patient, believing themselves possessed by the spirit of a dead doctor; and those who seem to perform real but paranormal operations which defy rational explanation.

Most of the world's psychic surgeons are in the Phillipines, and not all of them are honest – but one of the most sincere and hard-working is Tony Agpaoa. Witnesses to his healing sessions say the flesh just opens up to his touch as though he holds an invisible scalpel. Agpaoa has demonstrated this cutting effect by moving his finger past inanimate objects – like this bandage [1] – which cannot be said to be suffering from auto-suggestion.

The moment Agpaoa touches a patient blood appears everywhere. Agpaoa inserts his hand or fingers and within seconds emerges with a lump of tissue said to be causing the patient's problem [2-4 and 5-7]. After the operation Agpaoa again passes his hands over the wound, which heals instantly leaving no scar. Sometimes it is all so quick it is hard for all present to believe what they have seen.

Several well-publicized attempts to expose psychic surgeons have done little to clarify the situation, alleging the use of sleight of hand to conceal blood and bits of flesh which they pretend to remove from the patient's body. These dramatic tricks are said to do nothing more than reinforce a self-cure by auto-suggestion – but trick or not, genuine cures are surely welcome. Contrary to the exposés, many responsible people – among them Andrija Puharich, himself a doctor and mentor to Uri Geller – have had eye operations or lumps and tumours successfully removed in this way.

MIND OVER MATTER

Fire Immunity. Licking a white hot iron bar [1] is readily explained – all you need is speed, courage and the Leidenfrost effect, by which moisture on the tongue is vaporized to form an insulating layer of steam.

The man in this photo [2] is hypnotized and ordered not to feel the flame beneath his palm. The word 'hypnosis' itself explains little since the mechanism by which blisters and burns are prevented from appearing – is far from understood.

Perhaps a form of self-hypnosis occurs in the firewalks of the following pages. Many of them are conducted while in ecstasy, but it is clear the effects go beyond mere 'hypnosis'. These men [3, 4] are members of the Free Pentecostal Holiness Church of the poor backwoods communities among the southern slopes of the Allegheny Mountains, in the USA. At frequent revival meetings some members dramatize their faith in ecstasy, handling rattlesnakes, drinking strychnine and holding coal-oil torches to their hands and feet – usually without the slightest harm.

Complete lack of resistance to fire is very rare. Occasionally we hear of deaths like that of John Irving Bentley, 92, a retired doctor of Coudersport, Pennsylvania, most of whose remains were swiftly and utterly consumed by fire in 1966 [5]. The fire must have been incredibly fierce to do this, but where it came from, what fueled it, and how it was confined to such a small area of damage may remain unanswered as long as the existence of 'spontaneous combustion' is officially denied.

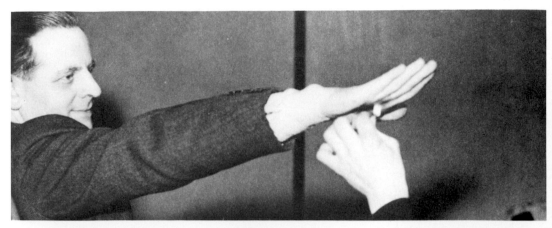

118

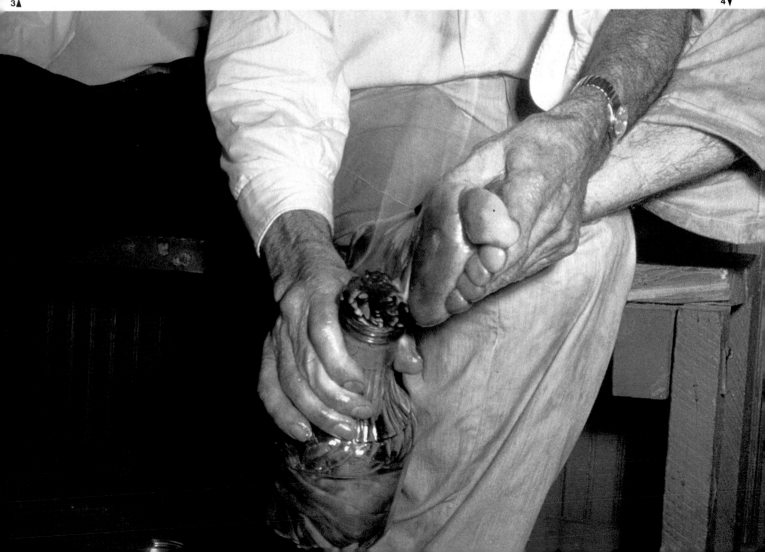

Firewalking. Andrew Lang, the great folklorist, long ago showed that firewalking rituals are universal, and usually vestiges of an ancient local religion superceded by the great religions of today.

Mysteriously, immunity can often be conferred on ordinary and unprepared members of the crowd by the priest, ascetic or shaman officiating, as happened to this spectator at a demonstration in New Delhi, India [1].

Next to the Polynesian firewalks (see p.122) the best known take place in Hindu communities, like this ceremony at Pietermaritzburg, South Africa [2] at a festival for the goddess Marraman; or this one in Singapore [3]. The largest of these celebrations takes place in the temple complex at Kataragama, in southern Sri Lanka, in honour of the god Skanda and his wives [4].

Less well known are the pagan survivals incorporated into contemporary Christian cultures. At Langadas, Greece [5] villagers dance in glowing embers clutching icons of St Constantine and his mother St Helen; and a similar ritual is observed in the Spanish village of San Pedro Manrigue, near Soria [6] on the feast of St John in June.

MIND OVER MATTER

Firewalking. Of all the acts of firewalking, we think the most impressive is the stroll over hot stones performed frequently among the islands of Fiji. Not only are the feet in firm contact with the glowing rocks which are very much hotter than embers of wood or coal, but they are also without the admittedly slight protection of layers of ash. Reason suggests that the walkers would be horribly burned or killed in the first few steps, but they survive without harm to walk over the almost molten rocks again and again.

The ceremonies had their origin in ancient Polynesian magical traditions. A rare demonstration was given by Chief Terrii Pao, whose kahuna magic included the use of leaves of the sacred ti plant [1].

The colour sequence was shot on the island of Beqa by English journalist, Charles Parr. The stones were cooked all day in a huge pit fueled by logs [2]. By evening the stones are white hot and the islanders in traditional dress stroll without the slightest discomfort [3]. Parr spoke to one of the firewalkers – a Fijian, named Isoe – before and after the event, who had been crossing the hot rocks regularly for eight years. It was difficult to believe that these feet [4] had been pressed against white hot rock the night before. What is even more astonishing is that this event has lost most of its religious significance – it is now a miracle performed weekly for tourists.

1

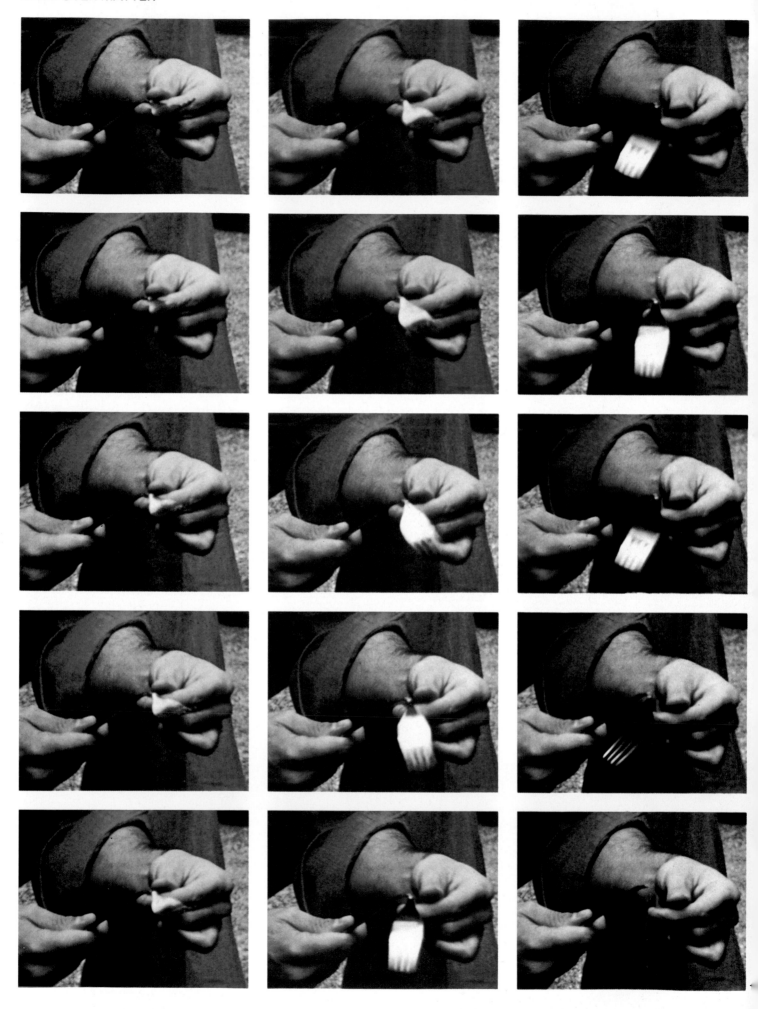

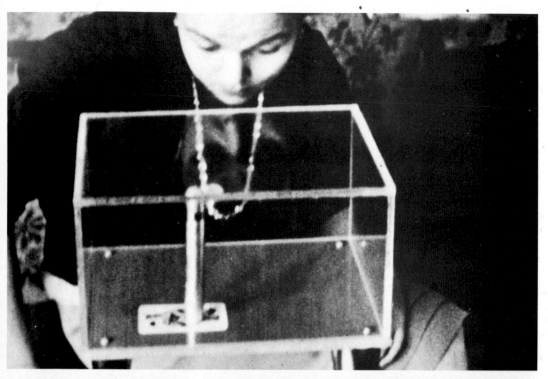

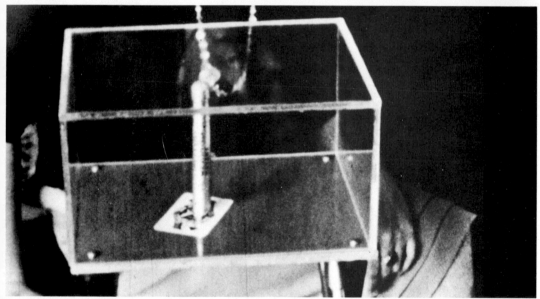

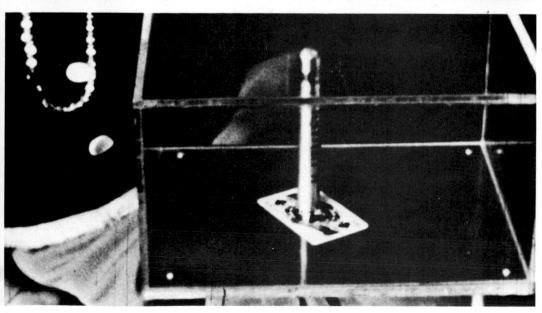

Spoonbenders. Israeli, Uri Geller became a celebrity overnight in 1973 with his startling demonstration on British TV, stroking a fork until it became soft and broke. In June 1973, James Bolen, editor of *Psychic* magazine, made a Super 8 ciné film, at close range, of a fork in Geller's hands [1]. The fork becomes visibly pliable at one point and simply falls apart. Microscopic examination of the fractured surfaces revealed traces of localized melting, as if under intense heat.

After Geller appeared on TV, many people came forward claiming similar abilities, and some of the younger ones were tested by Prof. John Hasted, at Birkbeck College, University of London. One of Hasted's exhibits is this glass sphere with one tiny hole in it, full of paperclips twisted and elongated by the concentration of 10-year-old Stephen North [2].

Perhaps some of the most remarkable examples of psychokinesis concern a Russian housewife, Ninel Kulagina, since her discovery in 1964. In the late 1960s Kulagina was filmed many times moving non-magnetic objects, placed under a protective plastic cover, at her mental command, as in this experiment using a cigar tube balanced on a playing card [3-5].

2

Table Turning. Tables flew in the presence of the Italian physical medium Francesco Carancini [1]. At the close of the 19th century investigations switched to Carancini's contemporary and countrywoman, Eusapia Palladino, arguably the most powerful medium on record. Much of her fame was due to the controversy and feuds among scientists that came in the wake of her demonstrations in Europe, Britain and America. However there is little doubt that Palladino did produce many authentic phenomena. This photo [2] taken in the 1890s was probably torn up by a frustrated sceptic.

Conversely, there was never any imputation of fraud against the unassuming London medium Jack Webber (see also p.74 and p.130). At least two of his table levitations, which occurred without planning or warning, were successfully photographed by Leon Isaacs, who had devised an infra-red flashgun system. This round table weighing 45lbs (20kg) took off in February 1939 [3]. At a sitting on 24 May 1939, a table that a moment before was resting in the space to Webber's right [4], danced in mid-air over the head of *Sunday Pictorial* reporter Bernard Gray (to the right of the picture) accounting for his apprehensive flinch.

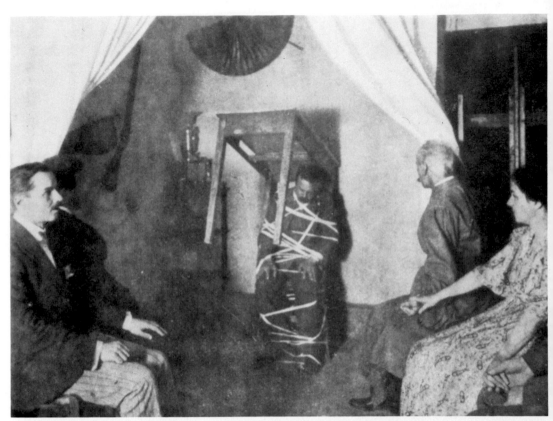

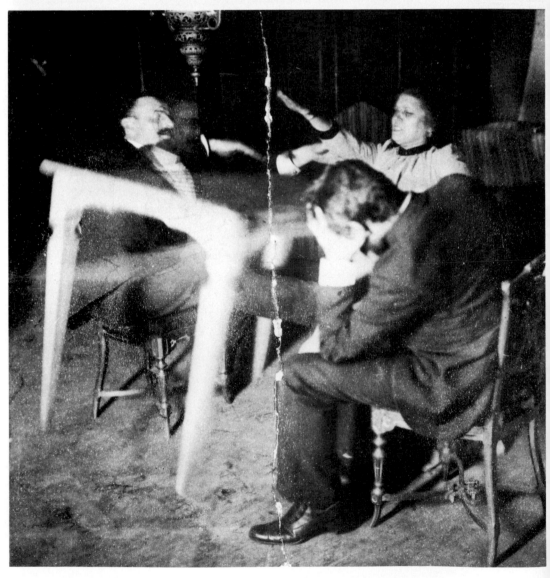

MIND OVER MATTER

Levitation of Objects. The spontaneous flight of objects during séances is well known – like this flying trumpet from a 1928 sitting of Guy L'Estrange, in Yarrow, Scotland [1]. (See also p.126.)

More impressive are the levitations of objects under the apparent control of the human will. The young Polish medium, Stanislawa Tomczyk, demonstrated her powers to the satisfaction of Professors Julien Ochorowicz and Theodor Flournoy and Baron Schrenck-Notzing. In 1908-9, Miss Tomczyk levitated a matchbox and scissors [2, 3] watched at close quarters by Ochorowicz.

Nearly 80 years later these feats of psychokinesis have been matched, and some say excelled, by the astonishing Russian mediums, Boris Ermolaev [4] and Ninel Kulagina [5]. (See also p.125.)

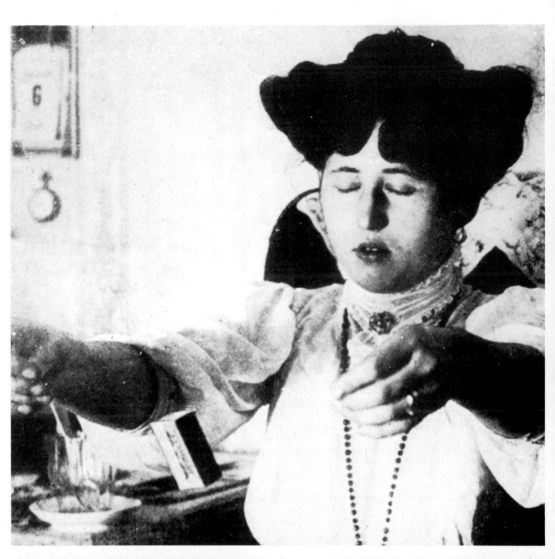

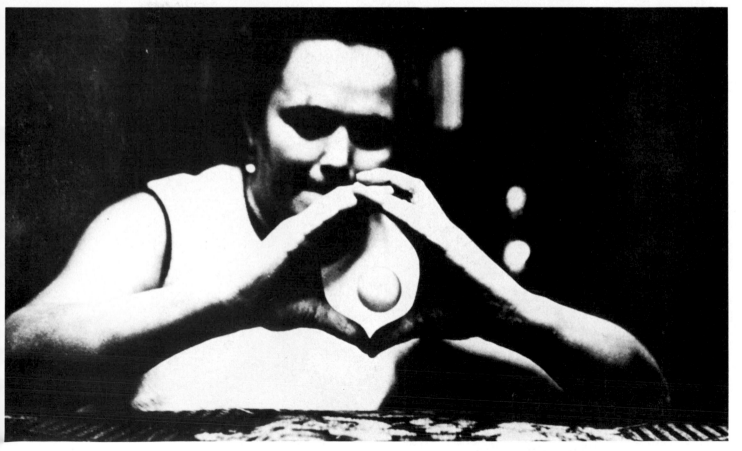

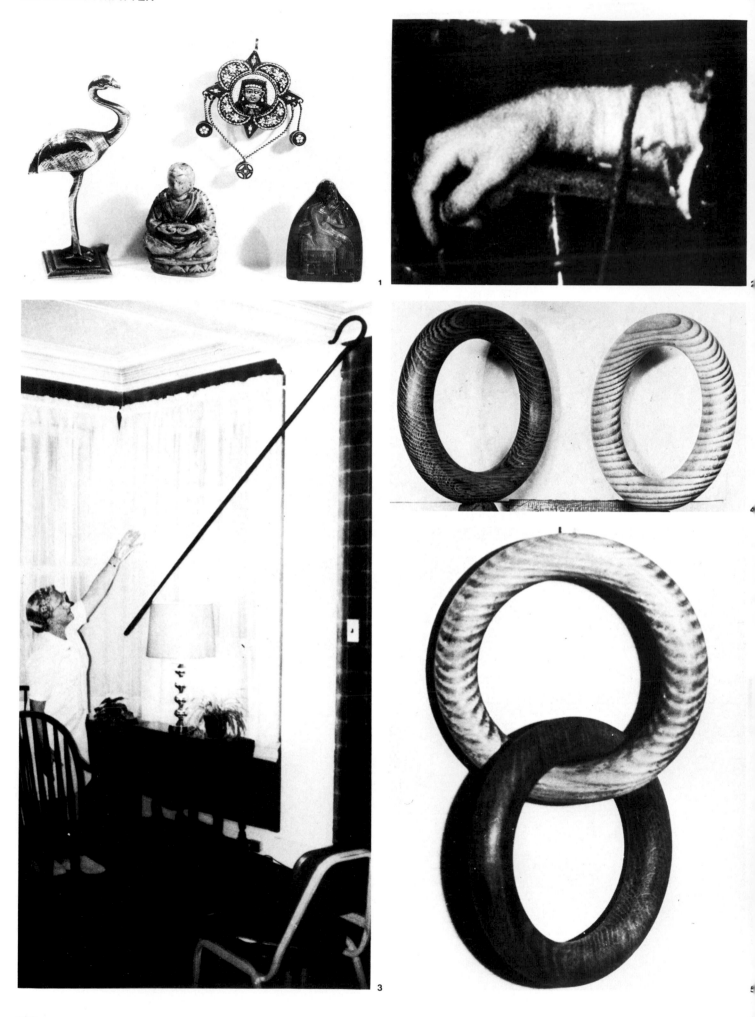

Apports. Frequently poltergeist attacks (see pp. 136-143) or mediumistic phenomena involve apports, mysteriously transported objects.

Jack Webber's séances (see also p.74 and p.126) included reliable instances of teleportation of small ornaments [1]. Here [2] a small brass bird appeared by the medium's bound arm, and fell to the floor seconds after a spirit guide ordered the photo taken.

Eileen Roberts, one of Britain's prominent spiritualists, visited the First Spiritualist Temple, in Boston, Massachusetts, in the autumn of 1979. After a long day's work she and her colleagues found a seven foot shepherd's crook firmly wedged near the ceiling [3]. It was normally kept in another room and somehow got itself into this predicament, without setting off an alarm-beam.

At the turn of the century, Sir Oliver Lodge supplied these rings made of different woods [4] to a medium. When they became mysteriously interlocked [5], Lodge declared it "a blow to materialism."

Satya Sai Baba, a modern Indian saint, revered as an incarnation of god, materializes extraordinary quantities of *vibhuti* (sacred ash), which drop from his fingers as a blessing [6]. Sai Baba also materializes *lingams,* egg-shaped stones, symbols of the Eternal, on the feast of Mahashivratri. On this occasion the *lingam* contained a star and crescent design [7]; within another was a cup-shaped flame [8] which changed colour frequently.

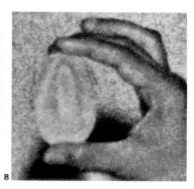

8

MIND OVER MATTER

Levitation. A remarkable performance of public levitation was observed in 1936 by an English tea plantation manager in southern India, P. T. Plunkett. The fakir's name was Subbayah Pullavar and he had practised obscure austerities for 20 years.

The stick was carefully examined by the audience before being stuck into the ground and wrapped in a sheet [1]. The fakir lay down near it and began his trance meditation [2], while a makeshift tent was quickly put up around him [3].

After a short while the tent was dismantled to reveal the fakir floating calmly in mid-air [4-6], his hand resting lightly on the wrapped stick. For four minutes Plunkett and his friend took photographs from all angles; then the procedure was reversed.

Plunkett, who had witnessed the act twice before, is convinced no mechanism lay concealed in the tent and stick. In the bright sunshine the sheets were thin and movement within easily discernible. Besides, he adds, he could see the man "slowly descend, still in a horizontal position."

1

4

6 ▶

Levitation. Photographs of human levitations are very rare and none are without their criticism. In each of the following cases we have the additional testimonies of many witnesses to genuine acts of levitation.

Firstly we have Colin Evans [1] who gave demonstrations to spiritualist meetings in the 1930s. He would float above the heads of the audience in darkness, only visible by luminous tapes on his hands and shoes[2].

The Italian medium Amadee Zuccarini, much earlier than Evans, was photographed levitating many times, but this was the only example we could find [3], presumably one of his tests for Prof. C. Murani at Milan Polytechnic. Zuccarini, like Evans, claimed the light from the magnesium flash destroyed his power of flight, so any photo would naturally reveal him falling.

Before his death, in 1951, Carlos Mirabelli, a Brazilian medium of Italian extraction, was believed to have accomplished every kind of mediumistic feat. He was seen to levitate many times, and this photo [4] shows him hovering near a high ceiling, sometime in the 1940s. While researching Mirabelli for his book on Brazil's psychic phenomena, *The Flying Cow,* Guy Lyon Playfair discovered the scene of the levitation. His photo [5] taken in 1973, shows the room redecorated and fitted with a partition, but still identifiable by the same ceiling light fitting, and the small light and dark windows on the back wall.

MIND OVER MATTER

Poltergeists. The range of phenomena usually attributed to spiritualism may appear in a spontaneous outbreak called a poltergeist haunting – which centres on an unwitting victim, often at puberty.

In 1965, an ordinary cane stick, which normally stood in a corner of 14-year-old Michael Collindridge's bedroom, in Barnsley, Yorkshire, became celebrated for its antics. Family and investigators saw and heard the stick leap about the room, tapping out pop tunes unaided [1]. It only happened if Michael was present, but he was watched closely and could not have done it by trickery.

The renowned psychic researcher, Harry Price, investigated the case of Alan Rhodes, 12, who in December 1945 lived with his grandmother in Crawley, Surrey. Price tied Alan's wrists to the bed as a precaution against fraud [2]. The clock and the box [3] were later found transported, the clock to the bed [4] and the box to the bed's foot [5, inset].

A classical example of a poltergeist-haunted youth came to light in 1925, when a Rumanian peasant girl, Eleonore Zugun, aged 12, was brought to London by Countess Wassilko-Serecki. A distinguished panel of researchers saw that Eleonore was an unconscious agent of apport phenomena (see p.130). More bizarre were the curious stigmata which would appear on the girl's skin [6, 7] while the girl believed she was being scratched and bitten by an invisible devil.

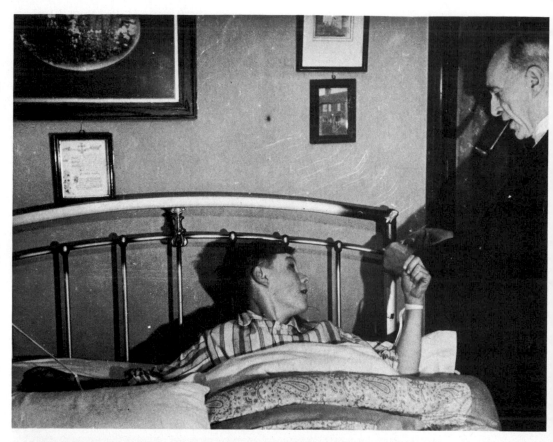

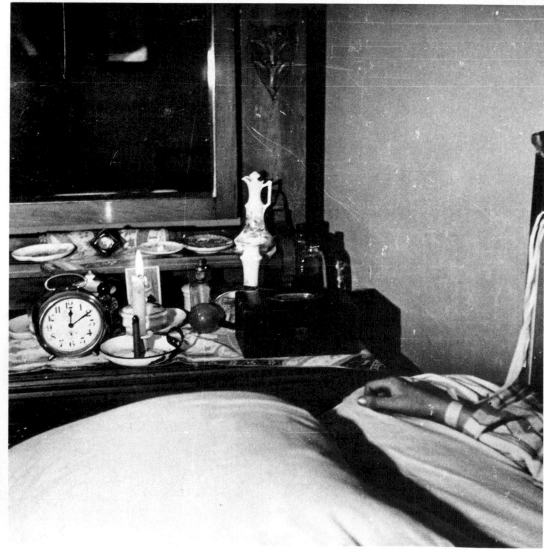

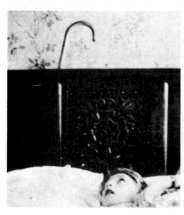

1

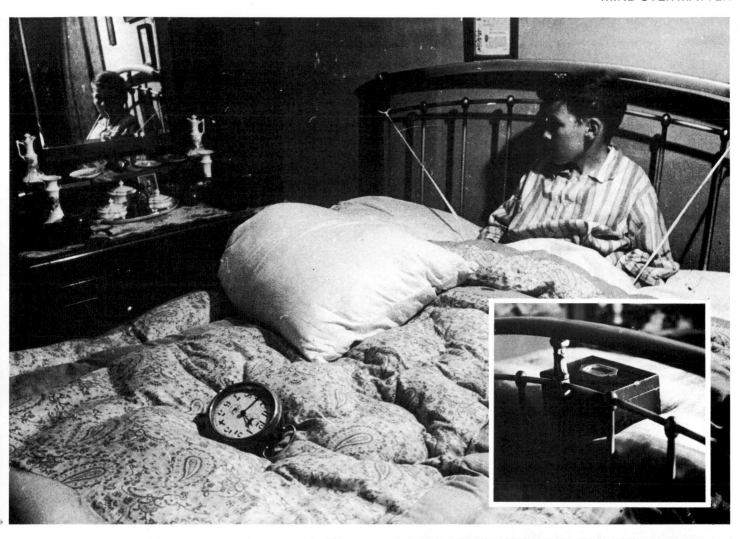

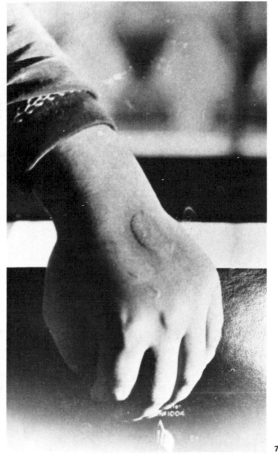

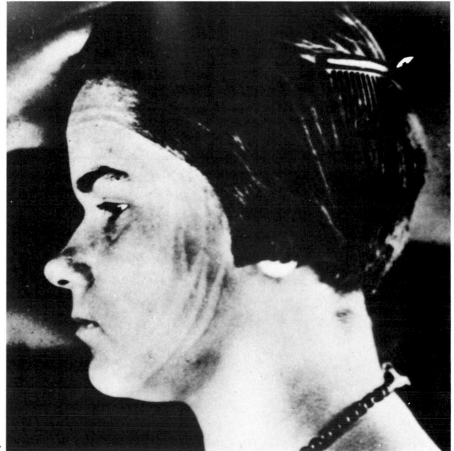

7

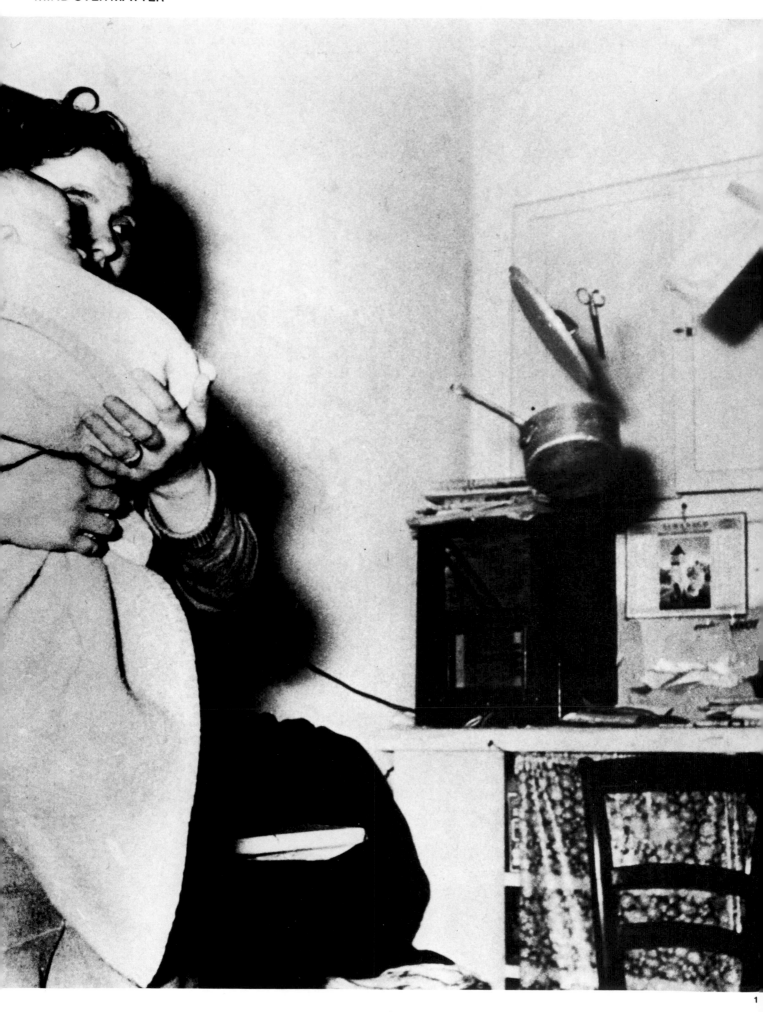

1

Poltergeists. Poltergeists are not restricted to plaguing adolescents. In June 1955, the focus of a French case was a mother, Teresa Costa, 24, and her baby [1]. The Costas were a poor family, living at St Jean de Maurienne, near the border with Italy, and were nearly driven from their home by the noises and flying household goods. This rare photograph of a poltergeist in action was taken by a visiting reporter.

In 1976 a poltergeist pest at a horticultural centre in Bromley, South London, centred on a 50-year-old man. Among the noises, movements and apports, were showers of sulphate of ammonia, used as fertilizer, one heap of which developed this face [2].

Poltergeists can also be responsible for the classical haunted-house type of case. One of the most famous of these was Borley Rectory, on the border of Suffolk and Essex. It was investigated by Harry Price between 1929, and 1939 when it was gutted by fire. Later the house was bulldozed and a photographer covering the story found he had inadvertently snapped an inexplicably flying brick [3] – a fitting end to the enigma.

Poltergeists are also characterized by their inscrutable indulgence in meaningful coincidences. In 1973, Dr Berthold Schwarz's wife, Ardis, became concerned about her father, near death in a Minneapolis nursing home. Suddenly a cup and saucer fell from a secure place to the kitchen floor – the saucer was broken and one fragment pointed to the word 'Dad' on the unharmed cup [4].

Poltergeists. Opinions about the origins of poltergeists differ among researchers, ranging from a belief in spirits to a link with emotional disturbances, usually during adolescence. A recent case highlighted the controversy and incidentally provided the first clear colour pictures of a poltergeist in action, taken by professional photographer Graham Morris.

The incident began in August 1977, with loud hammerings on the inside walls of a house in Enfield, London, occupied by Margaret Harper, 47, and her children, Rose, 13, Janet, 11, Pete, 10 and Jimmy, 7 (all pseudonyms). Within a week the Society for Psychical Research was called in, and investigators stayed with the case almost continuously for nearly two years until the family were re-housed. Furniture would be overturned, household objects hurled through the air, doors opened and closed, and the girls levitated. There were inexplicable fires, apparitions, strange flows of water, apports and invisible assaults. The phenomena seemed to centre on the two girls, but particularly on Janet, from whom issued a disembodied voice, which researcher Guy Playfair describes as "hoarse, rasping, and uncannily loud."

Playfair, and Maurice Grosse, who stayed longest with the case, are convinced of the genuineness of most of what they recorded.

Our photographs show: a pillow thrown to the floor while another flies through the air [1-3]; bedclothes which suddenly surged upwards towards a closed window, falling back as the curtain billowed and twisted on its own [4-6]. On the next two pages we show a few of the occasions Janet was lifted from her bed and hurled through the air [7-10]. And finally a photo unique in our experience – Janet, in a stupor after a Valium injection, was found mysteriously on top of a radio [11, inset bottom].

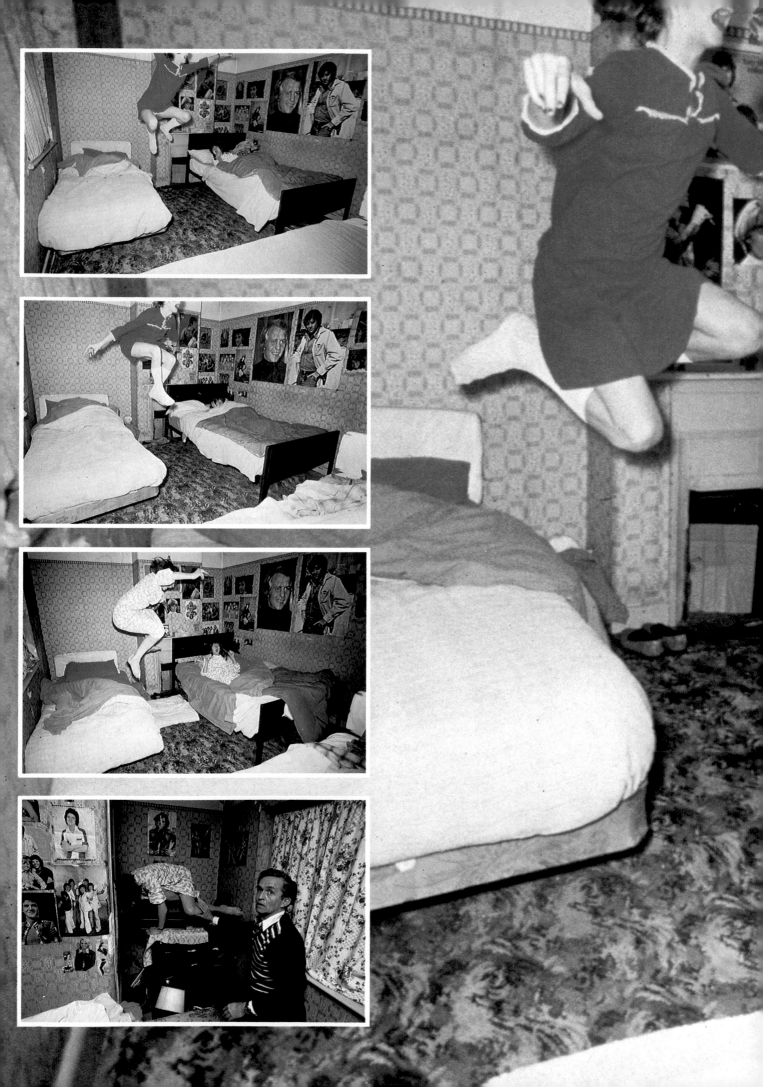

PICTURE CREDITS

WHERE TO SEND YOUR PHOTOGRAPHS

Do not send your photographs in the first instance, instead please send a brief description, with your address, to the authors at:

PHOTOGRAPHS OF THE UNKNOWN
c/o FORTEAN TIMES
9-12 ST. ANNES COURT
LONDON W1
ENGLAND

D.L.B. 21891– 1980